www.EffortlessMatn.com

... So Much More Online!

✓ FREE Math lessons

✓ More Math learning books!

✓ Mathematics Worksheets

✓ Online Math Tutors

Need a PDF version of this book?

Send email to: Info@EffortlessMath.com

Ace the TABE Math in 30 Days

The Ultimate Crash Course to Beat the TABE Math Test

By

Reza Nazari

& Ava Ross

Copyright © 2019

Reza Nazari & Ava Ross

All inquiries should be addressed to:

info@effortlessMath.com

www.EffortlessMath.com

ISBN–13: 978-1-970036-62-6

ISBN–10: 1-970036-62-1

Published by: Effortless Math Education

www.EffortlessMath.com

Description

The goal of this book is simple. It will help you incorporate the most effective method and the right strategies to prepare for the TABE Math test quickly and effectively.

Ace the TABE Math in 30 Days, which reflects the 2019 test guidelines and topics, is designed to help you hone your math skills, overcome your exam anxiety, and boost your confidence -- and do your best to defeat TABE Math Test. This TABE Math new edition has been updated to replicate questions appearing on the most recent TABE Math tests. This is a precious learning tool for TABE Math test takers who need extra practice in math to improve their TABE Math score. After reviewing this book, you will have solid foundation and adequate practice that is necessary to ace the TABE Math test. **This book is your ticket to ace the TABE Math!**

Ace the TABE Math in 30 Days provides students with the confidence and math skills they need to succeed on the TABE Math, providing a solid foundation of basic Math topics with abundant exercises for each topic. It is designed to address the needs of TABE test takers who must have a working knowledge of basic Math.

Inside the pages of this comprehensive book, students can learn math topics in a structured manner with a complete study program to help them understand essential math skills. It also has many exciting features, including:

- Content 100% aligned with the 2019 TABE test
- Written by TABE Math tutors and test experts
- Complete coverage of all TABE Math concepts and topics which you will be tested
- Step-by-step guide for all TABE Math topics
- Dynamic design and easy-to-follow activities
- Over 2,500 additional TABE math practice questions in both multiple-choice and grid-in formats with answers grouped by topic, so you can focus on your weak areas
- Abundant Math skill building exercises to help test-takers approach different question types that might be unfamiliar to them
- Exercises on different TABE Math topics such as integers, percent, equations, polynomials, exponents and radicals
- 2 full-length practice tests (featuring new question types) with detailed answers

Effortlessly and confidently follow the step-by-step instructions in this book to ace the TABE Math in a short period of time.

Ace the TABE Math in 30 Days is the only book you'll ever need to master Basic Math topics! It can be used as a self-study course - you do not need to work with a Math tutor. (It can also be used with a Math tutor).

You'll be surprised how fast you master the Math topics covering on TABE Math Test.

Ideal for self-study as well as for classroom usage.

About the Author

Reza Nazari is the author of more than 100 Math learning books including:
– **Math and Critical Thinking Challenges:** For the Middle and High School Student
– **GRE Math in 30 Days**
– **ASVAB Math Workbook 2018 - 2019**
– **Effortless Math Education Workbooks**
– **and many more Mathematics books …**

Reza is also an experienced Math instructor and a test–prep expert who has been tutoring students since 2008. Reza is the founder of Effortless Math Education, a tutoring company that has helped many students raise their standardized test scores—and attend the colleges of their dreams. Reza provides an individualized custom learning plan and the personalized attention that makes a difference in how students view math.

You can contact Reza via email at:
reza@EffortlessMath.com

Find Reza's professional profile at:
goo.gl/zoC9rJ

Contents

Day 1: Whole Numbers 11

    Rounding 12

    Whole Number Addition and Subtraction 13

    Whole Number Multiplication 14

    Whole Number Division 15

    Rounding and Estimates 16

    Answers – Day 1 17

Day 2: Fractions 18

    Simplifying Fractions 19

    Adding and Subtracting Fractions 20

    Multiplying and Dividing Fractions 21

    Answers – Day 2 22

Day 3: Mixed Numbers 23

    Adding Mixed Numbers 24

    Subtracting Mixed Numbers 25

    Multiplying Mixed Numbers 26

    Dividing Mixed Numbers 27

    Answers – Day 3 28

Day 4: Decimals 29

    Comparing Decimals 30

    Rounding Decimals 31

    Adding and Subtracting Decimals 32

    Multiplying and Dividing Decimals 33

    Answers – Day 4 34

Day 5: Factoring Numbers 35

    Factoring Numbers 36

    Greatest Common Factor 37

    Least Common Multiple 38

    Answers – Day 5 39

Day 6: Integers 40

    Adding and Subtracting Integers 41

Multiplying and Dividing Integers 42

Ordering Integers and Numbers 43

Answers – Day 6 44

Day 7: Order of Operations 45

Order of Operations 46

Integers and Absolute Value 47

Answers – Day 7 48

Day 8: Ratios 49

Simplifying Ratios 50

Proportional Ratios 51

Answers – Day 8 52

Day 9: Similarity and Proportions 53

Create a Proportion 54

Similarity and Ratios 55

Simple Interest 56

Answers – Day 9 57

Day 10: Percentage 58

Percentage Calculations 59

Percent Problems 60

Answers – Day 10 61

Day 11: Percent of Change 62

Percent of Increase and Decrease 63

Discount, Tax and Tip 64

Answers – Day 11 65

Day 12: Exponents and Variables 66

Multiplication Property of Exponents 67

Division Property of Exponents 68

Powers of Products and Quotients 69

Answers – Day 12 70

Day 13: Exponents and Roots 71

Zero and Negative Exponents 72

Negative Exponents and Negative Bases 73

Scientific Notation 74

Square Roots 75

Answers – Day 13 76

Day 14: Expressions and Variables 77

Simplifying Variable Expressions 78

Simplifying Polynomial Expressions 79

Translate Phrases into an Algebraic Statement 80

Answers – Day 14 81

Day 15: Evaluating Variables 82

The Distributive Property 83

Evaluating One Variable 84

Evaluating Two Variables 85

Combining like Terms 86

Answers – Day 15 87

Day 16: Equations and Inequalities 88

One–Step Equations 89

Multi–Step Equations 90

Graphing Single–Variable Inequalities 91

Answers – Day 16 92

Day 17: Solving Inequalities 93

One–Step Inequalities 94

Multi–Step Inequalities 95

Answers – Day 17 96

Day 18: Lines and Slope 97

Finding Slope 98

Graphing Lines Using Slope–Intercept Form 99

Graphing Lines Using Standard Form 100

Answers – Day 18 101

Day 19: Linear Equations and Inequalities 103

Writing Linear Equations 104

Graphing Linear Inequalities 105

Finding Midpoint 106

Finding Distance of Two Points 107

Answers – Day 19 108

Day 20: Polynomials 110

Writing Polynomials in Standard Form 111

Simplifying Polynomials 112

Adding and Subtracting Polynomials 113

Answers – Day 20 114

Day 21: Monomials Operations 115

Multiplying Monomials 116

Multiplying and Dividing Monomials 117

Multiplying a Polynomial and a Monomial 118

Answers – Day 21 119

Day 22: Polynomials Operations 120

Multiplying Binomials 121

Factoring Trinomials 122

Operations with Polynomials 123

Answers – Day 22 124

Day 23: System of Equations 125

Systems of Equations 126

Systems of Equations Word Problems 127

Answers – Day 23 128

Day 24: Triangles and Polygons 129

The Pythagorean Theorem 130

Triangles 131

Polygons 132

Answers – Day 24 133

Day 25: Circles, Trapezoids and Cubes 134

Circles 135

Trapezoids 136

Cubes 137

Answers – Day 25 138

Day 26: Rectangular Prisms and Cylinder 139

Rectangular Prisms...140

Cylinder 141

Answers – Day 26 142

Day 27: Statistics 143

Mean, Median, Mode, and Range of the Given Data 144

Histograms 145

Answers – Day 27 146

Day 28: Data and Probability 147

Pie Graph...148

Probability Problems 149

Answers – Day 28 150

Day 29: Time to Test 151

Complete TABE Battery Math Practice Test 2019 153

Complete TABE Battery Math Practice Test Answers and Explanations 170

Day 30: A Realistic TABE Math Test 181

Complete TABE Battery Math Practice Test 2019 182

Complete TABE Battery Math Practice Test Answers and Explanations 200

Day 1: Whole Numbers

Math Topics that you'll learn today:

- ✓ Rounding
- ✓ Whole Number Addition and Subtraction
- ✓ Whole Number Multiplication and Division
- ✓ Rounding and Estimates

"If people do not believe that mathematics is simple, it is only because they do not realize how complicated life is."

— John von Neumann

Rounding

Step-by-step guide:

Rounding is putting a number up or down to the nearest whole number or the nearest hundred, etc.

✓ *First, find the place value you'll round to.*
✓ *Find the digit to the right of the place value you're rounding to. If it is 5 or bigger, add 1 to the place value you're rounding to and put zero for all digits on its right side. If the digit to the right of the place value is less than 5, keep the place value and put zero for all digits to the right.*

Examples:

1) Round 64 to the nearest ten.

The place value of ten is 6. The digit on the right side is 4 (which is less than 5). Keep 6 and put zero for the digit on the right side. The answer is 60. 64 rounded to the nearest ten is 60, because 64 is closer to 60 than to 70.

2) Round 694 to the nearest hundred.

694 rounded to the nearest hundred is 700, because the digit on the right side of hundred place is 9. Add 1 to 6 and put zeros for other digits. The answer is 700.

✍ *Round each number to the nearest ten.*

1) 84 = ____   4) 63 = ____
2) 70 = ____   5) 79 = ____
3) 47 = ____   6) 55 = ____

✍ *Round each number to the nearest hundred.*

7) 185 = ____   10) 109 = ____
8) 254 = ____   11) 222 = ____
9) 729 = ____   12) 311 = ____

Whole Number Addition and Subtraction

Step-by-step guide:

- ✓ *Line up the numbers.*
- ✓ *Start with the unit place. (ones place)*
- ✓ *Regroup if necessary.*
- ✓ *Add or subtract the tens place.*
- ✓ *Continue with other digits.*

Examples:

1) Find the sum. $285 + 145 = ?$

First line up the numbers: $\begin{array}{r} 285 \\ +\,145 \\ \hline \end{array}$ $\rightarrow$ Start with the unit place. (ones place) $5 + 5 = 10$,

Write 0 for ones place and keep 1, $\begin{array}{r} {\scriptstyle 1} \\ 285 \\ +\,145 \\ \hline 0 \end{array}$, Add the tens place and the digit 1 we kept:

$1 + 8 + 4 = 13$, Write 3 and keep 1, $\begin{array}{r} {\scriptstyle 1\,1} \\ 285 \\ +\,145 \\ \hline 30 \end{array}$

Continue with other digits $\rightarrow 1 + 2 + 1 = 4 \rightarrow \begin{array}{r} {\scriptstyle 1\,1} \\ 285 \\ +\,145 \\ \hline 430 \end{array}$

2) Find the difference. $976 - 453 = ?$

First line up the numbers: $\begin{array}{r} 976 \\ -\,453 \\ \hline \end{array}$, $\rightarrow$ Start with the unit place. $6 - 3 = 3$, $\begin{array}{r} 976 \\ -\,453 \\ \hline 3 \end{array}$,

Subtract the tens place. $7 - 5 = 2$, $\begin{array}{r} 976 \\ -\,453 \\ \hline 23 \end{array}$, Continue with other digits $\rightarrow 9 - 4 = 5$, $\begin{array}{r} 976 \\ -\,453 \\ \hline 523 \end{array}$

✎ *Find the sum or difference.*

1) $1,264 + 856 =$

2) $2,689 - 456 =$

3) $1,432 - 556 =$

4) $2,820 + 464 =$

5) $2,170 + 245 =$

6) $3,221 + 2,560 =$

7) $3,788 + 1,892 =$

8) $4,238 + 2,576 =$

Whole Number Multiplication

Step-by-step guide:

- ✓ Learn the times tables first! To solve multiplication problems fast, you need to memorize the times table. For example, 3 times 8 is 24 or 8 times 7 is 56.
- ✓ For multiplication, line up the numbers you are multiplying.
- ✓ Start with the ones place and regroup if necessary.
- ✓ Continue with other digits.

Examples:

1) Solve. $500 \times 30 = ?$

Line up the numbers: $\begin{array}{r} 500 \\ \times\,30 \\ \hline \end{array}$, start with the ones place $\rightarrow 0 \times 500 = 0$, $\begin{array}{r} 500 \\ \times\,30 \\ \hline 0 \end{array}$, Continue

with other digit which is 3. $\rightarrow 500 \times 3 = 1,500$, $\begin{array}{r} 500 \\ \times\,30 \\ \hline 1,5000 \end{array}$

2) Solve. $820 \times 25 = ?$

Line up the numbers: $\begin{array}{r} 820 \\ \times\,25 \\ \hline \end{array}$, start with the ones place $\rightarrow 5 \times 0 = 0$, $\begin{array}{r} 820 \\ \times\,25 \\ \hline 0 \end{array}$, $5 \times 2 = 10$,

write 0 and keep 1. $\begin{array}{r} 820 \\ \times\,25 \\ \hline 00 \end{array}$, $\rightarrow 5 \times 8 = 40$, add 1 to 40, the answer is 41. $\begin{array}{r} 820 \\ \times\,25 \\ \hline 4,100 \end{array}$

Now, write 0 in the next line and multiply 820 by 2, using the same process. (Since 2 is in the tens place, we need to write 0 before doing the operation). The answer is 16,400. Add 4,100 and 16,400. The answer is: $4,100 + 16,400 = 20,500$

✎ *Find the missing number.*

1) $24 \times 5 = $ _____
2) $28 \times 8 = $ _____
3) $360 \times 6 = $ _____
4) $500 \times 12 = $ _____

5) $144 \times 51 = $ _____
6) $238 \times 18 = $ _____
7) $362 \times 14 = $ _____
8) $238 \times 28 = $ _____

Whole Number Division

Step-by-step guide:

Division: A typical division problem: Dividend ÷ Divisor = Quotient

- In division, we want to find how many times a number (divisor) is contained in another number (dividend). The result in a division problem is the quotient.
✓ First, write the problem in division format. (dividend is inside; divisor is outside)

$$\text{Divisor} \overline{)\text{Dividend}}^{\text{Quotient}}$$

✓ Now, find how many times divisor goes into dividend. (if it is a big number, break the dividend into smaller numbers by choosing the appropriate number of digits from left. Start from the first digit on the left side of the divided and see if the divisor will go into it. If not, keep moving over one digit to the right in the dividend until you have a number the divisor will go into.
✓ Find number of times the divisor goes into the part of the dividend you chose.
✓ Write the answer above the digit in the dividend you are using and multiply it by the divisor and Write the product under the part of the dividend you are using, then subtract.
✓ Bring down the next digit in the dividend and repeat this process until you have nothing left to bring down.

Example: Solve. $234 \div 4 = ?$

$$4 \overline{)234}$$

✓ First, write the problem in division format.
✓ Start from left digit of the dividend. 4 doesn't go into 2. So, choose another digit of the dividend. It is 3.
✓ Now, find how many times 4 goes into 23. The answer is 5.
✓ Write 5 above the dividend part. 4 times 5 is 20. Write 20 below 23 and subtract. The answer is 3.

$$4 \overline{)234}^{5}$$

✓ Now bring down the next digit which is 4. How many times 4 goes into 34? The answer is 8. Write 8 above dividend. This is the final step since there is no other digit of the dividend to bring down. The final answer is 58 and the remainder is 2.

$$\begin{array}{r} 58 \\ 4 \overline{)234} \\ -20 \\ \hline 34 \\ -32 \\ \hline 2 \end{array}$$

✎ *Solve.*

1) $240 \div 5 = $ _____
2) $280 \div 4 = $ _____
3) $562 \div 8 = $ _____
4) $522 \div 9 = $ _____

5) $834 \div 8 = $ _____
6) $922 \div 12 = $ _____
7) $880 \div 15 = $ _____
8) $721 \div 22 = $ _____

Rounding and Estimates

Step-by-step guide:

Rounding and estimating are math strategies used for approximating a number. To estimate means to make a rough guess or calculation. To round means to simplify a known number by scaling it slightly up or down.

✓ To estimate a math operation, round the numbers.
✓ For 2-digit numbers, your usually can round to the nearest tens, for 3-digit numbers, round to nearest hundreds, etc.
✓ Find the answer.

Examples:

1) Estimate the sum by rounding each number to the nearest hundred. $153 + 426 =?$
   153 rounded to the nearest hundred is 200. 426 rounded to the nearest hundred is 400.
   Then: $200 + 400 = 600$

2) Estimate the result by rounding each number to the nearest ten. $38 - 26 = ?$
   38 rounded to the nearest ten is 40. 25 rounded to the nearest ten is 30.
   Then: $40 - 30 = 10$

✎ *Estimate the sum by rounding each number to the nearest ten.*

1) $14 + 68 =$ _____   4) $47 + 69 =$ _____

2) $82 + 12 =$ _____   5) $553 + 231 =$ _____

3) $43 + 66 =$ _____   6) $418 + 849 =$ _____

✎ *Estimate the product by rounding each number to the nearest ten.*

7) $55 \times 62 =$ _____   10) $18 \times 12 =$ _____

8) $14 \times 27 =$ _____   11) $62 \times 53 =$ _____

9) $34 \times 66 =$ _____   12) $41 \times 26 =$ _____

Answers – Day 1

Rounding

1) 80
2) 70
3) 50
4) 60

5) 80
6) 60
7) 200
8) 300

9) 700
10) 100
11) 200
12) 300

Whole Number Addition and Subtraction

1) 2,120
2) 2,233
3) 876

4) 3,284
5) 2,415
6) 5,781

7) 5,680
8) 6,814

Whole Number Multiplication

1) 120
2) 224
3) 2,160

4) 6,000
5) 7,344
6) 4,284

7) 5,068
8) 6,664

Whole Number Division

1) 48
2) 70
3) $45, r2$

4) 58
5) $104, 2$
6) $153, r4$

7) $58, r10$
8) $32, 17$

Rounding and Estimates

1) 80
2) 90
3) 110
4) 120

5) 780
6) 1,270
7) 3,600
8) 300

9) 2,100
10) 200
11) 3,000
12) 1,200

Day 2: Fractions

Math Topics that you'll learn today:

- ✓ Comparing Numbers

- ✓ Simplifying Fractions

- ✓ Adding and Subtracting Fractions

- ✓ Multiplying and Dividing Fractions

"A Man is like a fraction whose numerator is what he is and whose denominator is what he thinks of himself. The larger the denominator, the smaller the fraction." -Tolstoy

Simplifying Fractions

Step-by-step guide:

- ✓ Evenly divide both the top and bottom of the fraction by $2, 3, 5, 7, \ldots$ etc.
- ✓ Continue until you can't go any further.

Examples:

1) Simplify $\frac{12}{20}$.

To simplify $\frac{12}{20}$, find a number that both 12 and 20 are divisible by. Both are divisible by 4.

Then: $\frac{12}{20} = \frac{12 \div 4}{20 \div 4} = \frac{3}{5}$

2) Simplify $\frac{64}{80}$.

To simplify $\frac{64}{80}$, find a number that both 64 and 80 are divisible by. Both are divisible by 8 and 16. Then: $\frac{64}{80} = \frac{64 \div 8}{80 \div 8} = \frac{8}{10}$, 8 and 10 are divisible by 2, then: $\frac{8}{10} = \frac{4}{5}$

or $\frac{64}{80} = \frac{64 \div 16}{80 \div 16} = \frac{4}{5}$

✍ *Simplify each fraction.*

1) $\frac{9}{18} =$

2) $\frac{8}{10} =$

3) $\frac{6}{8} =$

4) $\frac{5}{20} =$

5) $\frac{18}{24} =$

6) $\frac{6}{9} =$

7) $\frac{12}{15} =$

8) $\frac{4}{16} =$

9) $\frac{18}{36} =$

10) $\frac{6}{42} =$

11) $\frac{13}{39} =$

12) $\frac{21}{28} =$

Adding and Subtracting Fractions

Step-by-step guide:

- ✓ For "like" fractions (fractions with the same denominator), add or subtract the numerators and write the answer over the common denominator.
- ✓ Find equivalent fractions with the same denominator before you can add or subtract fractions with different denominators.
- ✓ Adding and Subtracting with the same denominator:

$$\frac{a}{b} + \frac{c}{b} = \frac{a+c}{b} \quad , \quad \frac{a}{b} - \frac{c}{b} = \frac{a-c}{b}$$

- ✓ Adding and Subtracting fractions with different denominators:

$$\frac{a}{b} + \frac{c}{d} = \frac{ad+c}{bd} \quad , \quad \frac{a}{b} - \frac{c}{d} = \frac{ad-cb}{bd}$$

Examples:

1) Subtract fractions. $\frac{4}{5} - \frac{3}{5} =$

   For "like" fractions, subtract the numerators and write the answer over the common denominator. then: $\frac{4}{5} - \frac{3}{5} = \frac{1}{5}$

2) Subtract fractions. $\frac{2}{3} - \frac{1}{2} =$

   For "unlike" fractions, find equivalent fractions with the same denominator before you can add or subtract fractions with different denominators. Use this formula: $\frac{a}{b} - \frac{c}{d} = \frac{ad-cb}{bd}$

   $\frac{2}{3} - \frac{1}{2} = \frac{(2)(2)-(1)(3)}{3 \times 2} = \frac{4-3}{6} = \frac{1}{6}$

✎ *Find the sum or difference.*

1) $\frac{1}{3} + \frac{2}{3} =$

2) $\frac{1}{2} + \frac{1}{3} =$

3) $\frac{2}{5} + \frac{1}{2} =$

4) $\frac{3}{7} + \frac{2}{3} =$

5) $\frac{1}{2} - \frac{1}{3} =$

6) $\frac{4}{5} - \frac{2}{3} =$

7) $\frac{2}{3} - \frac{1}{6} =$

8) $\frac{3}{5} - \frac{1}{2} =$

9) $\frac{8}{9} - \frac{2}{5} =$

Multiplying and Dividing Fractions

Step-by-step guide:

- ✓ Multiplying fractions: multiply the top numbers and multiply the bottom numbers.
- ✓ Dividing fractions: Keep, Change, Flip
- ✓ Keep first fraction, change division sign to multiplication, and flip the numerator and denominator of the second fraction. Then, solve!

Examples:

1) Multiplying fractions. $\frac{5}{6} \times \frac{3}{4} =$

Multiply the top numbers and multiply the bottom numbers.

$\frac{5}{6} \times \frac{3}{4} = \frac{5 \times 3}{6 \times 4} = \frac{15}{24}$, simplify: $\frac{15}{24} = \frac{15 \div 3}{24 \div 3} = \frac{5}{8}$

2) Dividing fractions. $\frac{1}{4} \div \frac{2}{3} =$

Keep first fraction, change division sign to multiplication, and flip the numerator and denominator of the second fraction. Then: $\frac{1}{4} \times \frac{3}{2} = \frac{1 \times 3}{4 \times 2} = \frac{3}{8}$

✍ *Find the answers.*

1) $\frac{1}{2} \times \frac{3}{4} =$

2) $\frac{3}{5} \times \frac{2}{3} =$

3) $\frac{1}{4} \times \frac{2}{5} =$

4) $\frac{1}{6} \times \frac{4}{5} =$

5) $\frac{1}{5} \times \frac{1}{4} =$

6) $\frac{2}{5} \times \frac{1}{2} =$

7) $\frac{1}{2} \div \frac{1}{4} =$

8) $\frac{1}{3} \div \frac{1}{2} =$

9) $\frac{2}{5} \div \frac{1}{3} =$

10) $\frac{1}{4} \div \frac{2}{3} =$

11) $\frac{1}{5} \div \frac{3}{10} =$

12) $\frac{2}{7} \div \frac{1}{3} =$

Answers – Day 2

Simplifying Fractions

1) $\frac{1}{2}$

2) $\frac{4}{5}$

3) $\frac{3}{4}$

4) $\frac{1}{4}$

5) $\frac{3}{4}$

6) $\frac{2}{3}$

7) $\frac{4}{5}$

8) $\frac{1}{4}$

9) $\frac{1}{2}$

10) $\frac{1}{7}$

11) $\frac{1}{3}$

12) $\frac{3}{4}$

Adding and Subtracting Fractions

1) $\frac{3}{3}=1$

2) $\frac{5}{6}$

3) $\frac{9}{10}$

4) $\frac{23}{21}$

5) $\frac{1}{6}$

6) $\frac{2}{15}$

7) $\frac{1}{2}$

8) $\frac{1}{10}$

9) $\frac{22}{45}$

Multiplying and Dividing Fractions

1) $\frac{3}{8}$

2) $\frac{2}{5}$

3) $\frac{1}{10}$

4) $\frac{2}{15}$

5) $\frac{1}{20}$

6) $\frac{1}{5}$

7) 2

8) $\frac{2}{3}$

9) $\frac{6}{5}$

10) $\frac{3}{8}$

11) $\frac{2}{3}$

12) $\frac{6}{7}$

Day 3: Mixed Numbers

Math Topics that you'll learn today:

✓ Adding Mixed Numbers

✓ Subtracting Mixed Numbers

✓ Multiplying Mixed Numbers

✓ Dividing Mixed Numbers

"Wherever there is number, there is beauty." - Proclus

Adding Mixed Numbers

Step-by-step guide:

Use the following steps for both adding and subtracting mixed numbers.

- ✓ Add whole numbers of the mixed numbers.
- ✓ Add the fractions of each mixed number.
- ✓ Find the Least Common Denominator (LCD) if necessary.
- ✓ Add whole numbers and fractions.
- ✓ Write your answer in lowest terms.

Examples:

1) Add mixed numbers. $1\frac{3}{4} + 2\frac{3}{8} =$

Rewriting our equation with parts separated, $1 + \frac{3}{4} + 2 + \frac{3}{8}$, Solving the whole number parts $1 + 2 = 3$, Solving the fraction parts $\frac{3}{4} + \frac{3}{8}$, and rewrite to solve with the equivalent fractions.

$\frac{6}{8} + \frac{3}{8} = \frac{9}{8} = 1\frac{1}{8}$, then Combining the whole and fraction parts $3 + 1 + \frac{1}{8} = 4\frac{1}{8}$

2) Add mixed numbers. $1\frac{2}{3} + 4\frac{1}{6} =$

Rewriting our equation with parts separated, $1 + \frac{2}{3} + 4 + \frac{1}{6}$, Solving the whole number parts $1 + 4 = 5$, Solving the fraction parts $\frac{2}{3} + \frac{1}{6}$, and rewrite to solve with the equivalent fractions.

$\frac{2}{3} + \frac{1}{6} = \frac{5}{6}$, then Combining the whole and fraction parts $5 + \frac{5}{6} = 5\frac{5}{6}$

✎ *Find the sum.*

1) $2\frac{1}{2} + 1\frac{1}{3} =$

2) $6\frac{1}{2} + 3\frac{1}{2} =$

3) $2\frac{3}{8} + 3\frac{1}{8} =$

4) $4\frac{1}{2} + 1\frac{1}{4} =$

5) $1\frac{3}{7} + 1\frac{5}{14} =$

6) $6\frac{5}{12} + 3\frac{3}{4} =$

7) $5\frac{1}{2} + 8\frac{3}{4} =$

8) $3\frac{7}{8} + 3\frac{1}{3} =$

9) $3\frac{3}{9} + 7\frac{6}{11} =$

Subtracting Mixed Numbers

Step-by-step guide:

Use the following steps for both adding and subtracting mixed numbers.

- ✓ Subtract the whole number of second mixed number from whole number of the first mixed number.
- ✓ Subtract the second fraction from the first one.
- ✓ Find the Least Common Denominator (LCD) if necessary.
- ✓ Add the result of whole numbers and fractions.
- ✓ Write your answer in lowest terms.

Examples:

1) Subtract. $5\frac{2}{3} - 2\frac{1}{4} =$

Rewriting our equation with parts separated, $5 + \frac{2}{3} - 2 - \frac{1}{4}$

Solving the whole number parts $5 - 2 = 3$, Solving the fraction parts, $\frac{2}{3} - \frac{1}{4} = \frac{8-3}{12} = \frac{5}{12}$

Combining the whole and fraction parts, $3 + \frac{5}{12} = 3\frac{5}{12}$

2) Subtract. $3\frac{4}{5} - 1\frac{1}{2} =$

Rewriting our equation with parts separated, $3 + \frac{4}{5} - 1 - \frac{1}{2}$

Solving the whole number parts $3 - 1 = 2$, Solving the fraction parts, $\frac{4}{5} - \frac{1}{2} = \frac{3}{10}$

Combining the whole and fraction parts, $2 + \frac{3}{10} = 2\frac{3}{10}$

✎ *Find the difference.*

1) $3\frac{1}{3} - 1\frac{1}{3} =$

2) $4\frac{1}{2} - 3\frac{1}{2} =$

3) $5\frac{1}{2} - 2\frac{1}{4} =$

4) $6\frac{1}{6} - 5\frac{1}{3} =$

5) $8\frac{1}{2} - 1\frac{1}{10} =$

6) $9\frac{1}{2} - 2\frac{1}{4} =$

7) $9\frac{1}{5} - 5\frac{1}{6} =$

8) $14\frac{3}{10} - 13\frac{1}{3} =$

9) $19\frac{2}{3} - 11\frac{5}{8} =$

Multiplying Mixed Numbers

Step-by-step guide:

   ✓ Convert the mixed numbers to improper fractions. (improper fraction is a fraction in which the top number is bigger than bottom number)

   ✓ Multiply fractions and simplify if necessary.

$$a\frac{c}{b} = a + \frac{c}{b} = \frac{ab+c}{b}$$

Examples:

1) Multiply mixed numbers. $3\frac{2}{3} \times 2\frac{1}{2} =$

Converting mixed numbers to fractions, $3\frac{2}{3} = \frac{11}{3}$ and $2\frac{1}{2} = \frac{5}{2}$.

$\frac{11}{3} \times \frac{5}{2}$, Applying the fractions formula for multiplication, $\frac{11\times5}{3\times2} = \frac{55}{6} = 9\frac{1}{6}$

2) Multiply mixed numbers. $4\frac{3}{5} \times 2\frac{1}{3} =$

Converting mixed numbers to fractions, $\frac{23}{5} \times \frac{7}{3}$, Applying the fractions formula for multiplication, $\frac{23\times7}{5\times3} = \frac{161}{15} = 10\frac{11}{15}$

✎ *Find the product.*

1) $4\frac{1}{3} \times 2\frac{1}{5} =$

2) $3\frac{1}{2} \times 3\frac{1}{4} =$

3) $5\frac{2}{5} \times 2\frac{1}{3} =$

4) $2\frac{1}{2} \times 1\frac{2}{9} =$

5) $3\frac{4}{7} \times 2\frac{3}{5} =$

6) $7\frac{2}{3} \times 2\frac{2}{3} =$

7) $9\frac{8}{9} \times 8\frac{3}{4} =$

8) $2\frac{4}{7} \times 5\frac{2}{9} =$

9) $5\frac{2}{5} \times 2\frac{3}{5} =$

10) $3\frac{5}{7} \times 3\frac{5}{6} =$

Dividing Mixed Numbers

Step-by-step guide:

- ✓ Convert the mixed numbers to improper fractions.
- ✓ Divide fractions and simplify if necessary.

$$a\frac{c}{b} = a + \frac{c}{b} = \frac{ab+c}{b}$$

Examples:

1) Find the quotient. $2\frac{1}{2} \div 1\frac{1}{5} =$

   Converting mixed numbers to fractions, $\frac{5}{2} \div \frac{6}{5}$, Applying the fractions formula for multiplication, $\frac{5 \times 5}{2 \times 6} = \frac{25}{12} = 2\frac{1}{12}$

2) Find the quotient. $4\frac{3}{4} \div 3\frac{4}{5} =$

   Converting mixed numbers to fractions, $\frac{19}{4} \div \frac{19}{5}$, Applying the fractions formula for multiplication, $\frac{19 \times 5}{4 \times 19} = \frac{95}{76} = 1\frac{1}{4}$

✍ *Find the quotient.*

1) $1\frac{2}{3} \div 3\frac{1}{3} =$

2) $2\frac{1}{4} \div 1\frac{1}{2} =$

3) $10\frac{1}{2} \div 1\frac{2}{3} =$

4) $3\frac{1}{6} \div 4\frac{2}{3} =$

5) $4\frac{1}{8} \div 2\frac{1}{2} =$

6) $2\frac{1}{10} \div 2\frac{3}{5} =$

7) $1\frac{4}{11} \div 1\frac{1}{4} =$

8) $9\frac{1}{2} \div 9\frac{2}{3} =$

9) $8\frac{3}{4} \div 2\frac{2}{5} =$

10) $12\frac{1}{2} \div 9\frac{1}{3} =$

Answers – Day 3

Adding Mixed Numbers

1) $3\frac{5}{6}$

2) 10

3) $5\frac{1}{2}$

4) $5\frac{3}{4}$

5) $2\frac{11}{14}$

6) $10\frac{1}{6}$

7) $14\frac{1}{4}$

8) $7\frac{5}{24}$

9) $10\frac{29}{33}$

Subtract Mixed Numbers

1) 2

2) 1

3) $3\frac{1}{4}$

4) $\frac{5}{6}$

5) $7\frac{2}{5}$

6) $7\frac{1}{4}$

7) $4\frac{1}{30}$

8) $\frac{29}{30}$

9) $8\frac{1}{24}$

Multiplying Mixed Numbers

1) $9\frac{8}{15}$

2) $11\frac{3}{8}$

3) $12\frac{3}{5}$

4) $3\frac{1}{18}$

5) $9\frac{2}{7}$

6) $20\frac{4}{9}$

7) $86\frac{19}{36}$

8) $13\frac{3}{7}$

9) $14\frac{1}{25}$

10) $14\frac{5}{21}$

Dividing Mixed Numbers

1) $\frac{1}{2}$

2) $1\frac{1}{2}$

3) $6\frac{3}{10}$

4) $\frac{19}{28}$

5) $1\frac{13}{20}$

6) $\frac{21}{26}$

7) $1\frac{1}{11}$

8) $\frac{57}{58}$

9) $3\frac{31}{48}$

10) $1\frac{19}{56}$

Day 4: Decimals

Math Topics that you'll learn today:

- ✓ Comparing Decimals

- ✓ Rounding Decimals

- ✓ Adding and Subtracting Decimals

- ✓ Multiplying and Dividing Decimals

"Do not worry about your difficulties in mathematics. I can assure you mine are still greater." ~ Albert Einstein

Comparing Decimals

Step-by-step guide:

Decimals: is a fraction written in a special form. For example, instead of writing $\frac{1}{2}$ you can write 0.5.

For comparing decimals:

✓ Compare each digit of two decimals in the same place value.
✓ Start from left. Compare hundreds, tens, ones, tenth, hundredth, etc.
✓ To compare numbers, use these symbols:
- Equal to $=$,   Less than $<$,   Greater than $>$
  Greater than or equal $\geq$,   Less than or equal $\leq$

Examples:

1) Compare 0.20 and 0.02.

   0.20 *is greater than* 0.02, because the tenth place of 0.20 is 2, but the tenth place of 0.02 is zero. Then: $0.20 > 0.02$

2) Compare 0.0210 and 0.110.

   $0.0.110$ *is greater than* 0.0210, because the tenth place of 0.110 is 1, but the tenth place of 0.0210 is zero. Then: $0.0210 < 0.110$

✍ *Write the correct comparison symbol (>, < or =).*

1) $0.50 \;\square\; 0.050$

2) $0.025 \;\square\; 0.25$

3) $2.060 \;\square\; 2.07$

4) $1.75 \;\square\; 1.07$

5) $4.04 \;\square\; 0.440$

6) $3.05 \;\square\; 3.5$

7) $5.05 \;\square\; 5.050$

8) $1.02 \;\square\; 1.1$

9) $2.45 \;\square\; 2.125$

10) $0.932 \;\square\; 0.0932$

11) $3.15 \;\square\; 3.150$

12) $0.718 \;\square\; 0.89$

Rounding Decimals

Step-by-step guide:

- ✓ We can round decimals to a certain accuracy or number of decimal places. This is used to make calculation easier to do and results easier to understand, when exact values are not too important.
- ✓ First, you'll need to remember your place values: For example:

$$12.4567$$

1: tens	2: ones	4: tenths
5: hundredths	6: thousandths	7: tens thousandths

- ✓ To round a decimal, find the place value you'll round to.
- ✓ Find the digit to the right of the place value you're rounding to. If it is 5 or bigger, add 1 to the place value you're rounding to and remove all digits on its right side. If the digit to the right of the place value is less than 5, keep the place value and remove all digits on the right.

Examples:

1) Round 2.1837 to the thousandth place value.

First look at the next place value to the right, (tens thousandths). It's 7 and it is greater than 5. Thus add 1 to the digit in the thousandth place.

Thousandth place is 3. $\rightarrow 3 + 1 = 4$, then, the answer is 2.184

2) 2.1837 rounded to the nearest hundredth.

First look at the next place value to the right of thousandths. It's 3 and it is less than 5, thus remove all the digits to the right. Then, the answer is 2.18.

✍ *Round each decimal to the nearest whole number.*

1) 23.18	3) 14.45	5) 3.95
2) 8.6	4) 7.5	6) 56.7

✍ *Round each decimal to the nearest tenth.*

7) 22.652	9) 47.847	11) 16.184
8) 30.342	10) 82.88	12) 71.79

Adding and Subtracting Decimals

Step-by-step guide:

✓ Line up the numbers.

✓ Add zeros to have same number of digits for both numbers if necessary.

✓ Add or subtract using column addition or subtraction.

Examples:

1) Add. $2.5 + 1.24 =$

First line up the numbers: $\begin{array}{r} 2.5 \\ +\ 1.24 \\ \hline \end{array}$ → Add zeros to have same number of digits for both

numbers. $\begin{array}{r} 2.50 \\ +\ 1.24 \\ \hline \end{array}$, Start with the hundredths place. $0 + 4 = 4$, $\begin{array}{r} 2.50 \\ +\ 1.24 \\ \hline 4 \end{array}$, Continue with tenths

place. $5 + 2 = 7$, $\begin{array}{r} 2.50 \\ +\ 1.24 \\ \hline .74 \end{array}$. Add the ones place. $2 + 1 = 3$, $\begin{array}{r} 2.50 \\ +\ 1.24 \\ \hline 3.74 \end{array}$

2) Subtract decimals. $4.67 + 2.15 = \begin{array}{r} 4.67 \\ -\ 2.15 \\ \hline \end{array}$

Start with the hundredths place. $7 - 5 = 2$, $\begin{array}{r} 4.67 \\ -\ 2.15 \\ \hline 2 \end{array}$, continue with tenths place. $6 - 1 = 5$

$\begin{array}{r} 4.67 \\ -\ 2.15 \\ \hline .52 \end{array}$, subtract the ones place. $4 - 2 = 2$, $\begin{array}{r} 4.67 \\ -\ 2.15 \\ \hline 2.52 \end{array}$.

✍ *Find the sum or difference.*

1) $31.13 - 11.45 =$

2) $35.25 + 24.47 =$

3) $73.50 + 22.78 =$

4) $56.67 - 44.39 =$

5) $71.47 + 16.25 =$

6) $68.99 - 53.61 =$

7) $66.24 - 23.11 =$

8) $39.75 + 12.85 =$

Multiplying and Dividing Decimals

Step-by-step guide:

For Multiplication:

✓ Ignore the decimal point and set up and multiply the numbers as you do with whole numbers.
Count the total number of decimal places in both of the factors.
Place the decimal point in the product.
For Division:

✓ If the divisor is not a whole number, move decimal point to right to make it a whole number. Do the same for dividend.

✓ Divide similar to whole numbers.

Examples:

1) Find the product. $0.50 \times 0.20 =$

Set up and multiply the numbers as you do with whole numbers. Line up the numbers: $\frac{50}{\times 20}$, Start with

the ones place → $50 \times 0 = 0$, $\frac{50}{\times 20}{0}$, Continue with other digits → $50 \times 2 = 100$, $\frac{50}{\times 20}{1,000}$, Count the

total number of decimal places in both of the factors. (4). Then Place the decimal point in the product.

Then: $\frac{0.50}{\times 0.20}{0.1000}$ → $0.50 \times 0.20 = 0.1$

2) Find the quotient. $1.20 \div 0.2 =$

The divisor is not a whole number. Multiply it by 10 to get 2. Do the same for the dividend to get 12.
Now, divide: $12 \div 2 = 6$. The answer is 6.

✎ *Find the product and quotient.*

1) $0.5 \times 0.4 =$

2) $2.5 \times 0.2 =$

3) $1.25 \times 0.5 =$

4) $0.75 \times 0.2 =$

5) $1.92 \times 0.8 =$

6) $0.55 \times 0.4 =$

7) $1.67 \div 100 =$

8) $52.2 \div 1,000 =$

9) $4.2 \div 2 =$

10) $8.6 \div 0.5 =$

11) $12.6 \div 0.2 =$

12) $16.5 \div 5 =$

Answers – Day 4

Comparing Decimals

1) >
2) <
3) <
4) >
5) >
6) <

7) =
8) <
9) >
10) >
11) =
12) <

Rounding Decimals

1) 23
2) 9
3) 14
4) 8

5) 4
6) 57
7) 22.7
8) 30.3

9) 47.8
10) 82.9
11) 16.2
12) 71.8

Adding and Subtracting Decimals

1) 19.68
2) 59.72
3) 96.28

4) 12.28
5) 87.72
6) 15.38

7) 43.13
8) 52.60

Multiplying and Dividing Decimals

1) 0.20
2) 0.50
3) 0.625
4) 0.15

5) 1.536
6) 0.22
7) 0.0167
8) 0.0522

9) 2.10
10) 17.2
11) 63
12) 3.3

Day 5: Factoring Numbers

Math Topics that you'll learn today:

- ✓ Factoring Numbers

- ✓ Greatest Common Factor

- ✓ Least Common Multiple

"The study of mathematics, like the Nile, begins in minuteness but ends in magnificence."

– Charles Caleb Colton

Factoring Numbers

Step-by-step guide:

- ✓ Factoring numbers means to break the numbers into their prime factors.
- ✓ First few prime numbers: $2, 3, 5, 7, 11, 13, 17, 19$

Examples:

1) List all positive factors of 12.

   Write the upside-down division:
   The second column is the answer.
   Then: $12 = 2 \times 2 \times 3$ or $12 = 2^2 \times 3$

12	2
6	2
3	3
1	

2) List all positive factors of 20.

   Write the upside-down division:
   The second column is the answer.
   Then: $20 = 2 \times 2 \times 5$ or $20 = 2^2 \times 5$

20	2
10	2
5	5
1	

✎ *List all positive factors of each number.*

1) 8	5) 25	9) 42
2) 9	6) 28	10) 48
3) 15	7) 26	11) 50
4) 16	8) 35	12) 36

Greatest Common Factor

Step-by-step guide:

- ✓ List the prime factors of each number.
- ✓ Multiply common prime factors.
- ✓ If there are no common prime factors, the GCF is 1.

Examples:

1) Find the GCF for 10 and 15.

The factors of 10 are: $\{1, 2, 5, 10\}$

The factors of 15 are: $\{1, 3, 5, 15\}$

There is 5 in common,

Then the greatest common factor is: 5.

2) Find the GCF for 8 and 20.

The factors of 8 are: $\{1, 2, 4, 8\}$

The factors of 20 are: $\{1, 2, 4, 5, 10, 20\}$

There is 2 and 4 in common.

Then the greatest common factor is: $2 \times 4 = 8$.

✍ *Find the GCF for each number pair.*

1) 4, 2	5) 5, 10	9) 5, 12
2) 3, 5	6) 6, 12	10) 4, 14
3) 2, 6	7) 7, 14	11) 15, 18
4) 4, 7	8) 6, 14	12) 12, 20

Least Common Multiple

Step-by-step guide:

✓ Least Common Multiple is the smallest multiple that 2 or more numbers have in common.

✓ How to find LCM: list out all the multiples of each number and then find the first one they have in common,

Examples:

1) Find the LCM for 3 and 4.

   Multiples of 3: $3, 6, 9, 12, 15, 18, 21, 24$

   Multiples of 4: $4, 8, 12, 16, 20, 24$

   $LCM = 12$

2) Find the LCM for 9 and 12.

   Multiples of 9: $9, 18, 27, 36, 45$

   Multiples of 12: $12, 24, 36, 48$

   $LCM = 36$

✍ *Find the LCM for each number pair.*

1) 3, 6	5) 6, 18	9) 4, 18
2) 5, 10	6) 10, 12	10) 9, 12
3) 6, 14	7) 4, 12	11) 12, 16
4) 8, 9	8) 5, 15	12) 15, 18

Answers – Day 5

Factoring Numbers

1) 1, 2, 4, 8
2) 1, 3, 9
3) 1, 3, 5, 15
4) 1, 2, 4, 8, 16
5) 1, 5, 25
6) 1, 2, 4, 7, 14, 28

7) 1, 2, 13, 26
8) 1, 5, 7, 35
9) 1, 2, 3, 6, 7, 14, 21, 42
10) 1, 2, 3, 4, 6, 8, 12, 16, 24, 48
11) 1, 2, 5, 10, 25, 50
12) 1, 2, 3, 4, 6, 9, 12, 18, 36

Greatest Common Factor

1) 2
2) 1
3) 2
4) 1
5) 5
6) 12

7) 7
8) 2
9) 1
10) 2
11) 3
12) 8

Least Common Multiple

1) 6
2) 10
3) 42
4) 72
5) 18
6) 60

7) 12
8) 15
9) 36
10) 36
11) 48
12) 90

Day 6: Integers

Math Topics that you'll learn today:

- ✓ Adding and Subtracting Integers

- ✓ Multiplying and Dividing Integers

- ✓ Ordering Integers and Numbers

Without mathematics, there's nothing you can do. Everything around you is mathematics. Everything around you is numbers." - Shakuntala Devi

Adding and Subtracting Integers

Step-by-step guide:

- ✓ Integers includes: zero, counting numbers, and the negative of the counting numbers. {... , − 3, − 2, − 1, 0, 1, 2, 3, ...}
- ✓ Add a positive integer by moving to the right on the number line.
- ✓ Add a negative integer by moving to the left on the number line.
- ✓ Subtract an integer by adding its opposite.

Examples:

1) Solve. $(-8) - (-5) =$

Keep the first number, and convert the sign of the second number to it's opposite. (change subtraction into addition. Then: $(-8) + 5 = -3$

2) Solve. $10 + (4 - 8) =$

First subtract the numbers in brackets, $4 - 8 = -4$

Then: $10 + (-4) = \rightarrow$ change addition into subtraction: $10 - 4 = 6$

✎ *Find each sum or difference.*

1) $12 + (-5) =$

2) $(-14) + (-18) =$

3) $8 + (-28) =$

4) $43 + (-12) =$

5) $(-7) + (-11) + 4 =$

6) $37 + (-16) + 12 =$

7) $(-12) - (-8) =$

8) $15 - (-20) =$

9) $(-11) - 25 =$

10) $30 - (-16) =$

11) $56 - (45 - 23) =$

12) $15 - (-4) - (-34) =$

Multiplying and Dividing Integers

Step-by-step guide:

Use these rules for multiplying and dividing integers:

- ✓ (negative) × (negative) = positive
- ✓ (negative) ÷ (negative) = positive
- ✓ (negative) × (positive) = negative
- ✓ (negative) ÷ (positive) = negative
- ✓ (positive) × (positive) = positive

Examples:

1) Solve. $(2 - 5) \times (3) =$

First subtract the numbers in brackets, $2 - 5 = -3 \rightarrow (-3) \times (3) =$

Now use this formula: (negative) × (positive) = negative
$(-3) \times (3) = -9$

2) Solve. $(-12) + (48 \div 6) =$

First divided 48 by 6 , the numbers in brackets, $48 \div 6 = 8$

$= (-12) + (8) = -12 + 8 = -4$

✎ *Find each product or quotient.*

1) $(-7) \times (-8) =$

2) $(-4) \times 5 =$

3) $5 \times (-11) =$

4) $(-5) \times (-20) =$

5) $-(2) \times (-8) \times 3 =$

6) $(12 - 4) \times (-10) =$

7) $16 \div (-4) =$

8) $(-25) \div (-5) =$

9) $(-40) \div (-8) =$

10) $64 \div (-8) =$

11) $(-49) \div 7 =$

12) $(-112) \div (-4) =$

Ordering Integers and Numbers

Step-by-step guide:

✓ When using a number line, numbers increase as you move to the right.
✓ When comparing two numbers, think about their position on number line. If one number is on the right side of another number, it is a bigger number. For example, -3 is bigger than -5 because it is on the right side of -5 on number line.

Examples:

1) Order this set of integers from least to greatest. $-2, 1, -5, -1, 2, 4$
   The smallest number is -5 and the largest number is 4.

   Now compare the integers and order them from greatest to least:
   $-5 < -2 < -1 < 1 < 2 < 4$

2) Order each set of integers from greatest to least. $10, -6, -2, 5, -8, 4$
   The largest number is 10 and the smallest number is -8.

   Now compare the integers and order them from least to greatest:
   $10 > 5 > 4 > -2 > -6 > -8$

✎ *Order each set of integers from least to greatest.*

1) $7, -9, -6, -1, 3$ ___, ___, ___, ___, ___, ___
2) $-4, -11, 5, 12, 9$ ___, ___, ___, ___, ___, ___
3) $18, -12, -19, 21, -20$ ___, ___, ___, ___, ___, ___
4) $-15, -25, 18, -7, 32$ ___, ___, ___, ___, ___, ___

✎ *Order each set of integers from greatest to least.*

5) $11, 16, -9, -12, -4$ ___, ___, ___, ___, ___, ___
6) $23, 31, -14, -20, 39$ ___, ___, ___, ___, ___, ___
7) $45, -21, -18, 55, -5$ ___, ___, ___, ___, ___, ___
8) $68, 81, -14, -10, 94$ ___, ___, ___, ___, ___, ___

Answers – Day 6

Adding and Subtracting Integers

1) 7
2) −32
3) −20
4) 31
5) −14
6) 33

7) −4
8) 35
9) −36
10) 46
11) 34
12) 53

Multiplying and Dividing Integers

1) 56
2) −20
3) −55
4) 100
5) 48
6) −80

7) −4
8) 5
9) 5
10) −8
11) −7
12) 28

Ordering Integers and Numbers

1) −9, −6, −1, 3, 7
2) −11, −4, 5, 9, 12
3) −20, −19, −12, 18, 21
4) −25, −15, −7, 18, 32

5) 16, 11, −4, −9, −12
6) 39, 31, 23, −14, −20
7) 55, 45, −5, −18, −21
8) 94, 81, 68, −10, −14

Day 7: Order of Operations

Math Topics that you'll learn today:

✓ Order of Operations

✓ Integers and Absolute Value

"Sometimes the questions are complicated and the answers are simple." - Dr. Seuss

Order of Operations

Step-by-step guide:

When there is more than one math operation, use PEMDAS:

- ✓ Parentheses
- ✓ Exponents
- ✓ Multiplication and Division (from left to right)
- ✓ Addition and Subtraction (from left to right)

Examples:

1) Solve. $(5 + 7) \div (3^2 \div 3) =$

First simplify inside parentheses: $(12) \div (9 \div 3) = (12) \div (3) =$
Then: $(12) \div (3) = 4$

2) Solve. $(11 \times 5) - (12 - 7) =$

First simplify inside parentheses: $(11 \times 5) - (12 - 7) = (55) - (5) =$

Then: $(55) - (5) = 50$

✍ *Evaluate each expression.*

1) $5 + (4 \times 2) =$

2) $13 - (2 \times 5) =$

3) $(16 \times 2) + 18 =$

4) $(12 - 5) - (4 \times 3) =$

5) $25 + (14 \div 2) =$

6) $(18 \times 5) \div 5 =$

7) $(48 \div 2) \times (-4) =$

8) $(7 \times 5) + (25 - 12) =$

9) $64 + (3 \times 2) + 8 =$

10) $(20 \times 5) \div (4 + 1) =$

11) $(-9) + (12 \times 6) + 15 =$

12) $(7 \times 8) - (56 \div 4) =$

Integers and Absolute Value

Step-by-step guide:

- ✓ To find an absolute value of a number, just find its distance from 0 on number line! For example, the distance of 12 and -12 from zero on number line is 12!

Examples:

1) Solve. $\frac{|-1|}{9} \times |5 - 8| =$

First find $|-18|$, →the absolute value of -18 is 18, then: $|-18| = 18$

$\frac{18}{9} \times |5 - 8| =$

Next, solve $|5 - 8|$, → $|5 - 8| = |-3|$, the absolute value of -3 is 3. $|-3| = 3$

Then: $\frac{18}{9} \times 3 = 2 \times 3 = 6$

2) Solve. $|10 - 5| \times \frac{|-2 \times 6|}{3} =$

First solve $|10 - 5|$, → $|10 - 5| = |5|$, the absolute value of 5 is 5, $|5| = 5$

$5 \times \frac{|-2 \times 6|}{3} =$

Now solve $|-2 \times 6|$, → $|-2 \times 6| = |-12|$, the absolute value of -12 is 12, $|-12| = 12$

Then: $5 \times \frac{12}{3} = 5 \times 4 = 20$

✎ *Evaluate the value.*

1) $8 - |2 - 14| - |-2| =$

2) $|-2| - \frac{|-1|}{2} =$

3) $\frac{|-3|}{6} \times |-6| =$

4) $\frac{|5 \times -3|}{5} \times \frac{|-20|}{4} =$

5) $|2 \times -4| + \frac{|-4|}{5} =$

6) $\frac{|-28|}{4} \times \frac{|-55|}{11} =$

7) $|-12 + 4| \times \frac{|-4 \times 5|}{2} =$

8) $\frac{|-10 \times 3|}{2} \times |-12| =$

Answers – Day 7

Order of Operations

1) 13
2) 3
3) 50
4) −5
5) 32
6) 18

7) −96
8) 48
9) 78
10) 20
11) 78
12) 42

Integers and Absolute Value

1) −6
2) −3
3) 36
4) 15

5) 16
6) 35
7) 80
8) 180

Day 8: Ratios

Math Topics that you'll learn today:

✓ Simplifying Ratios

✓ Proportional Ratios

Mathematics is the door and key to the sciences. ~ Roger Bacon

Simplifying Ratios

Step-by-step guide:

- ✓ Ratios are used to make comparisons between two numbers.
- ✓ Ratios can be written as a fraction, using the word "to", or with a colon.
- ✓ You can calculate equivalent ratios by multiplying or dividing both sides of the ratio by the same number.

Examples:

1) Simplify. $8: 4 =$

Both numbers 8 and 4 are divisible by 4, $\Rightarrow 8 \div 4 = 2, 4 \div 4 = 1,$

Then: $8: 4 = 2: 1$

2) Simplify. $\frac{12}{36} =$

Both numbers 12 and 36 are divisible by 12, $\Rightarrow 12 \div 12 = 1, 36 \div 12 = 3,$

Then: $\frac{12}{36} = \frac{1}{3}$

✎ *Reduce each ratio.*

1) $12: 8 =$ ___: ___

2) $2: 20 =$ ___: ___

3) $3: 36 =$ ___: ___

4) $8: 16 =$ ___: ___

5) $6: 100 =$ ___: ___

6) $10: 60 =$ ___: ___

7) $21: 49 =$ ___: ___

8) $20: 40 =$ ___: ___

9) $10: 50 =$ ___: ___

10) $14: 18 =$ ___: ___

11) $45: 27 =$ ___: ___

12) $49: 21 =$ ___: ___

Proportional Ratios

Step-by-step guide:

✓ A proportion means that two ratios are equal. It can be written in two ways:
$\frac{a}{b} = \frac{c}{d}$, $a : b = c : d$

✓ The proportion $\frac{a}{b} = \frac{c}{d}$ can be written as: $a \times d = c \times b$

Examples:

1) Solve this proportion for x. $\frac{4}{8} = \frac{5}{x}$

Use cross multiplication: $\frac{4}{8} = \frac{5}{x} \Rightarrow 4 \times x = 5 \times 8 \Rightarrow 4x = 40$

Divide to find x: $x = \frac{40}{4} \Rightarrow x = 10$

2) If a box contains red and blue balls in ratio of $2:3$ red to blue, how many red balls are there if 90 blue balls are in the box?

Write a proportion and solve. $\frac{2}{3} = \frac{x}{90}$
Use cross multiplication: $2 \times 90 = 3 \times x \Rightarrow 180 = 3x$
Divide to find x: $x = \frac{180}{3} \Rightarrow x = 60$

✍ *Solve each proportion.*

1) $\frac{2}{5} = \frac{14}{x}$, $x =$ ____

2) $\frac{1}{6} = \frac{7}{x}$, $x =$ ____

3) $\frac{3}{5} = \frac{27}{x}$, $x =$ ____

4) $\frac{1}{5} = \frac{x}{80}$, $x =$ ____

5) $\frac{3}{7} = \frac{x}{63}$, $x =$ ____

6) $\frac{1}{4} = \frac{13}{x}$, $x =$ ____

7) $\frac{7}{9} = \frac{56}{x}$, $x =$ ____

8) $\frac{6}{11} = \frac{42}{x}$, $x =$ ____

9) $\frac{4}{7} = \frac{x}{77}$, $x =$ ____

10) $\frac{5}{13} = \frac{x}{143}$, $x =$ ____

11) $\frac{7}{19} = \frac{x}{209}$, $x =$ ____

12) $\frac{3}{13} = \frac{x}{195}$, $x =$ ____

Answers – Day 8

Simplifying Ratios

1) 3 : 2
2) 1 : 10
3) 1 : 12
4) 1 : 2
5) 3 : 50
6) 1 : 6

7) 3 : 7
8) 1 : 2
9) 1 : 5
10) 7 : 9
11) 5 : 3
12) 7 : 3

Proportional Ratios

1) 35
2) 42
3) 45
4) 16
5) 27
6) 52

7) 72
8) 77
9) 44
10) 55
11) 77
12) 45

Day 9: Similarity and Proportions

Math Topics that you'll learn today:

✓ Create a Proportion

✓ Similarity and Ratios

✓ Simple Interest

Mathematics - the unshaken Foundation of Sciences, and the plentiful Fountain of Advantage to human affairs. –

Isaac Barrow

Create a Proportion

Step-by-step guide:

✓ A proportion contains two equal fractions! A proportion simply means that two fractions are equal.

✓ To create a proportion, simply find (or create) two equal fractions.

Examples:

1) Express ratios as a Proportion.
120 miles on 4 gallons of gas, how many miles on 1 gallon of gas?

First create a fraction: $\frac{120\ miles}{4\ gallons}$, and divide: $120 \div 4 = 30$

Then: 30 miles per gallon

2) State if this pair of ratios form a proportion. $\frac{3}{5}\ and\ \frac{24}{45}$

Use cross multiplication: $\frac{3}{5} = \frac{24}{45} \to 3 \times 45 = 5 \times 24 \to 135 = 120$, which is not correct.
Therefore, this pair of ratios doesn't form a proportion.

✎ *State if each pair of ratios form a proportion.*

1) $\frac{3}{10}\ and\ \frac{9}{30}$

2) $\frac{1}{2}\ and\ \frac{16}{32}$

3) $\frac{5}{6}\ and\ \frac{35}{42}$

4) $\frac{3}{7}\ and\ \frac{27}{72}$

5) $\frac{2}{5}\ and\ \frac{16}{45}$

6) $\frac{4}{9}\ and\ \frac{40}{81}$

7) $\frac{6}{11}\ and\ \frac{42}{77}$

8) $\frac{1}{6}\ and\ \frac{8}{48}$

9) $\frac{6}{17}\ and\ \frac{36}{85}$

10) $\frac{2}{7}\ and\ \frac{24}{86}$

11) $\frac{12}{19}\ and\ \frac{156}{247}$

12) $\frac{13}{21}\ and\ \frac{182}{294}$

Similarity and Ratios

Step-by-step guide:

✓ Two or more figures are similar if the corresponding angles are equal, and the corresponding sides are in proportion.

Examples:

1) A girl 160 cm tall, stands 360 cm from a lamp post at night. Her shadow from the light is 90 cm long. How high is the lamp post?

Write the proportion and solve for missing side.

$$\frac{\text{Smaller triangle height}}{\text{Smaller triangle base}} = \frac{\text{Bigger triangle height}}{\text{Bigger triangle base}}$$

$$\Rightarrow \frac{90cm}{160cm} = \frac{90+360cm}{x} \Rightarrow 90x = 160 \times 450 \Rightarrow x = 800 \; cm$$

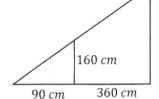

2) A tree 32 $feet$ tall casts a shadow 12 $feet$ long. Jack is 6 $feet$ tall. How long is Jack's shadow?

Write a proportion and solve for the missing number.

$$\frac{32}{12} = \frac{6}{x} \rightarrow 32x = 6 \times 12 = 72$$

$$32x = 72 \rightarrow x = \frac{72}{32} = 2.25$$

✎ Solve.

1) Two rectangles are similar. The first is 6 $feet$ wide and 20 $feet$ long. The second is 15 $feet$ wide. What is the length of the second rectangle? _____

2) Two rectangles are similar. One is 2.5 $meters$ by 9 $meters$. The longer side of the second rectangle is 22.5 $meters$. What is the other side of the second rectangle? _____

3) A building casts a shadow 24 ft long. At the same time a girl 5 ft tall casts a shadow 2 ft long. How tall is the building? _____

4) The scale of a map of Texas is 2 $inches$: 45 $miles$. If you measure the distance from Dallas to Martin County as 14.4 $inches$, approximately how far is Martin County from Dallas? _____

Simple Interest

Step-by-step guide:

✓ Simple Interest: The charge for borrowing money or the return for lending it. To solve a simple interest problem, use this formula:

Interest = principal × rate × time ⇒ $I = p \times r \times t$

Examples:

1) Find simple interest for $450 investment at 7% for 8 years.

Use Interest formula: $I = prt$

$P = \$450$, $r = 7\% = \frac{7}{100} = 0.07$ and $t = 8$

Then: $I = 450 \times 0.07 \times 8 = \$252$

2) Find simple interest for $5,200 at 4% for 3 years.

Use Interest formula: $I = prt$

$P = \$5,200$, $r = 4\% = \frac{4}{100} = 0.04$ and $t = 3$

Then: $I = 5,200 \times 0.04 \times 3 = \$624$

✍ *Determine the simple interest for these loans.*

1) $1,300 at 5% for 6 years. $ _____

2) $5,400 at 3.5% for 6 months. $ _____

3) $600 at 4% for 9 months. $ _____

4) $24,000 at 5.5% for 5 years. $ _____

5) $15,600 at 3% for 2 years. $ _____

6) $1,200 at 5.5% for 4 years. $ _____

7) $1,600 at 4.5% for 9 months. $ _____

8) $12,000 at 2.2% for 5 years. $ _____

Answers – Day 9

Create a Proportion

1) Yes
2) Yes
3) Yes
4) No
5) No
6) No

7) Yes
8) Yes
9) No
10) No
11) Yes
12) Yes

Similarity and ratios

1) 50 feet
2) 6.25 meters
3) 60 feet
4) 324 miles

Simple Interest

1) $390.00
2) $94.50
3) $18.00
4) $6,600.00

5) $936.00
6) $264.00
7) $54
8) $1,320.00

Day 10: Percentage

Math Topics that you'll learn today:

✓ Percentage Calculations

✓ Percent Problems

Mathematics is no more computation than typing is literature.

~ John Allen Paulos

Percentage Calculations

Step-by-step guide:

- ✓ Percent is a ratio of a number and 100. It always has the same denominator, 100. Percent symbol is %.
- ✓ Percent is another way to write decimals or fractions. For example:
$$40\% = 0.40 = \frac{40}{100} = \frac{2}{5}$$
- ✓ Use the following formula to find part, whole, or percent:
$$\text{part} = \frac{\text{percent}}{100} \times \text{whole}$$

Examples:

1) What is 10% of 45? Use the following formula: $\text{part} = \frac{\text{percent}}{100} \times \text{whole}$

$\text{part} = \frac{10}{100} \times 45 \rightarrow \text{part} = \frac{1}{10} \times 45 \rightarrow \text{part} = \frac{45}{10} \rightarrow \text{part} = 4.5$

2) What is 15% of 24? Use the percent formula: $\text{part} = \frac{\text{percent}}{100} \times \text{whole}$

$\text{part} = \frac{15}{100} \times 24 \rightarrow \text{part} = \frac{360}{100} \rightarrow \text{part} = 3.6$

✎ *Calculate the given percent of each value.*

1) 2% of 50 = ____
2) 10% of 30 = ____
3) 20% of 25 = ____
4) 50% of 80 = ____
5) 40% of 200 = ____
6) 20% of 45 = ____
7) 35% of 20 = ____
8) 12% of 400 = ____
9) 40% of 90 = ____
10) 25% of 812 = ____
11) 32% of 600 = ____
12) 87% of 500 = ____

Percent Problems

Step-by-step guide:

- ✓ In each percent problem, we are looking for the base, or part or the percent.
- ✓ Use the following equations to find each missing section.
  - ○ Base = Part ÷ Percent
  - ○ Part = Percent × Base
  - ○ Percent = Part ÷ Base

Examples:

1) 1.2 is what percent of 24?

In this problem, we are looking for the percent. Use the following equation:
$$Percent = Part ÷ Base → Percent = 1.2 ÷ 24 = 0.05 = 5\%$$

2) 20 is 5% of what number?

Use the following formula: $Base = Part ÷ Percent → Base = 20 ÷ 0.05 = 400$
20 is 5% of 400.

✎ *Solve each problem.*

1) 20 is what percent of 50? ____%

2) 18 is what percent of 90? ____%

3) 12 is what percent of 15? ____%

4) 16 is what percent of 200? ____%

5) 24 is what percent of 800? ____%

6) 48 is what percent of 4,00? ____%

7) 90 is 12 percent of what number? ____

8) 24 is 8 percent of what? ____

9) 60 is 15 percent of what number? ____

10) 42 *is 12 percent of what?* ___

11) 11 *is 25 percent of what?* ___

12) 8 *is 12.5 percent of what?* ___

Answers – Day 10

Percentage Calculations

1) 1
2) 3
3) 5
4) 40
5) 80
6) 9

7) 7
8) 48
9) 36
10) 203
11) 192
12) 435

Percent Problems

1) 40%
2) 20%
3) 80%
4) 8%
5) 3%
6) 12%

7) 750
8) 300
9) 400
10) 350
11) 44
12) 64

Day 11: Percent of Change

Math Topics that you'll learn today:

✓ Percent of Increase and Decrease

✓ Discount, Tax and Tip

Mathematics is a great motivator for all humans. Because its career starts with zero and it never end (infinity).

Percent of Increase and Decrease

Step-by-step guide:

To find the percentage of increase or decrease:
- ✓ New Number – Original Number
- ✓ The result ÷ Original Number × 100
- ✓ If your answer is a negative number, then this is a percentage decrease. If it is positive, then this is a percent of increase.

Examples:

1) Increased by 50%, the numbers 84 becomes:

First find 50% of 84 → $\frac{50}{100} \times 84 = \frac{50 \times 84}{100} = 42$

Then: $84 + 42 = 126$

2) The price of a shirt increases from \$10 to \$14. What is the percent increase?

First: $14 - 10 = 4$

4 is the result. Then: $4 \div 10 = \frac{4}{10} = 0.4 = 40\%$

✍ *Solve each percent of change word problem.*

1) Bob got a raise, and his hourly wage increased from \$12 to \$15. What is the percent increase? _____ %

2) The price of a pair of shoes increases from \$20 to \$32. What is the percent increase? ____ %

3) At a coffeeshop, the price of a cup of coffee increased from \$1.20 to \$1.44. What is the percent increase in the cost of the coffee? _____ %

4) 6 *cm* are cut from a 24 *cm* board. What is the percent decrease in length? _____ %

5) In a class, the number of students has been increased from 18 to 27. What is the percent increase? _____ %

6) The price of gasoline rose from \$2.40 to \$2.76 in one month. By what percent did the gas price rise? _____ %

7) A shirt was originally priced at \$48. It went on sale for \$38.40. What was the percent that the shirt was discounted? _____ %

Discount, Tax and Tip

Step-by-step guide:

- ✓ Discount = Multiply the regular price by the rate of discount
- ✓ Selling price = original price – discount
- ✓ Tax: To find tax, multiply the tax rate to the taxable amount (income, property value, etc.)
- ✓ To find tip, multiply the rate to the selling price.

Examples:

1) With an 10% discount, Ella was able to save $20 on a dress. What was the original price of the dress?

$10\% \ of \ x = \ 20, \frac{10}{100} \times x = \ 20, x = \frac{100 \times 20}{10} = 200$

2) Sophia purchased a sofa for $530.40. The sofa is regularly priced at $624. What was the percent discount Sophia received on the sofa?

Use this formula: $percent = Part \div base = 530.40 \div 624 = 0.85 = 85\%$

Therefore, the discount is: $100\% - 85\% = 15\%$

✍ *Find the selling price of each item.*

1) Original price of a computer: $500

   Tax: 6%, Selling price: $_____

2) Original price of a laptop: $350

   Tax: 8%, Selling price: $_____

3) Original price of a sofa: $800

   Tax: 7%, Selling price: $_____

4) Original price of a car: $18,500

   Tax: 8.5%, Selling price: $_____

5) Original price of a Table: $250

   Tax: 5%, Selling price: $_____

6) Original price of a house: $250,000

   Tax: 6.5% Selling price: $_____

7) Original price of a tablet: $400

   Discount: 20%, Selling price: $_____

8) Original price of a chair: $150

   Discount: 15%, Selling price: $_____

9) Original price of a book: $50

   Discount: 25%, Selling price: $_____

10) Original price of a cellphone: $500

   Discount: 10%, Selling price: $_____

Answers – Day 11

Percent of Increase and Decrease

1) 25%
2) 60%
3) 20%
4) 25%

5) 50%
6) 15%
7) 20%

Markup, Discount, and Tip

1) $530.00
2) $378.00
3) $856.00
4) $20,072.50
5) $262.50

6) $266,250
7) $320.00
8) $127.50
9) $37.50
10) $450.00

Day 12:
Exponents and Variables

Math Topics that you'll learn today:

- ✓ Multiplication Property of Exponents

- ✓ Division Property of Exponents

- ✓ Powers of Products and Quotients

Mathematics is an art of human understanding. ~ William Thurston

Multiplication Property of Exponents

Step-by-step guide:

- ✓ Exponents are shorthand for repeated multiplication of the same number by itself. For example, instead of 2×2, we can write 2^2. For $3 \times 3 \times 3 \times 3$, we can write 3^4
- ✓ In algebra, a variable is a letter used to stand for a number. The most common letters are: $x, y, z, a, b, c, m,$ and n.
- ✓ Exponent's rules: $x^a \times x^b = x^{a+b}$, $\frac{x^a}{x^b} = x^{a-b}$

$$(x^a)^b = x^{a \times b}, \qquad (xy)^a = x^a \times y^a , (\frac{a}{b})^c = \frac{a^c}{b^c}$$

Examples:

1) Multiply. $-2x^5 \times 7x^3 =$

   Use Exponent's rules: $x^a \times x^b = x^{a+b} \rightarrow x^5 \times x^3 = x^{5+3} = x^8$

   Then: $-2x^5 \times 7x^3 = -14x^8$

2) Multiply. $(x^2y^4)^3 =$

   Use Exponent's rules: $(x^a)^b = x^{a \times b}$. Then: $(x^2y^4)^3 = x^{2 \times 3}y^{4 \times 3} = x^6y^{12}$

✎ *Simplify and write the answer in exponential form.*

1) $x^4 \times 3x =$

2) $x \times 2x^2 =$

3) $5x^4 \times 5x^4 =$

4) $2yx^2 \times 2x =$

5) $3x^4 \times y^2x^4 =$

6) $y^2x^3 \times y^5x^2 =$

7) $4yx^3 \times 2x^2y^3 =$

8) $6x^2 \times 6x^3y^4 =$

9) $3x^4y^5 \times 7x^2y^3 =$

10) $7x^2 \ ^5 \times 9xy^3 =$

11) $7xy^4 \times 4x^3y^3 =$

12) $3x^5y^3 \times 8x^2y^3 =$

Division Property of Exponents

Step-by-step guide:

- ✓ For division of exponents use these formulas: $\frac{x^a}{x^b} = x^{a-b}$, $x \neq 0$

$$\frac{x^a}{b} = \frac{1}{x^{b-a}}, x \neq 0, \qquad \frac{1}{x^b} = x^{-b}$$

Examples:

1) Simplify. $\frac{4x^3y}{36x^2y^3} =$

First cancel the common factor: $4 \to \frac{4x^3y}{36x^2y^3} = \frac{x^3y}{9x^2y^3}$

Use Exponent's rules: $\frac{x^a}{x^b} = x^{a-b} \to \frac{x^3}{x^2} = x^{3-b}$

Then: $\frac{4x^3y}{36\ ^2y^3} = \frac{xy}{9y^3} \to$ now cancel the common factor: $y \to \frac{xy}{9y^3} = \frac{xy}{9y^2}$

2) Divide. $\frac{2x^{-5}}{9x^{-2}} =$

Use Exponent's rules: $\frac{x^a}{x^b} = \frac{1}{x^{b-a}} \to \frac{x^{-5}}{x^{-2}} = \frac{1}{x^{-2-(-5)}} = \frac{1}{x^{-2+5}} = \frac{1}{x^3}$

Then: $\frac{2x^{-5}}{9x^{-2}} = \frac{2}{9x^3}$

✎ **Simplify.**

1) $\frac{3^4 \times 3^7}{3^2 \times 3^8} =$

2) $\frac{5x}{10x^3} =$

3) $\frac{3x^3}{2x^5} =$

4) $\frac{12x^3}{14x^6} =$

5) $\frac{12x^3}{9y^8} =$

6) $\frac{25xy^4}{5x^6y^2} =$

7) $\frac{2x^4}{7x} =$

8) $\frac{16\ ^2y^8}{4x^3} =$

9) $\frac{12x^4}{15x^7y^9} =$

10) $\frac{12yx^4}{10yx^8} =$

11) $\frac{16x^4y}{9x^8y^2} =$

12) $\frac{5x^8}{20x^8} =$

Powers of Products and Quotients

Step-by-step guide:

✓ For any nonzero numbers a and b and any integer x, $(ab)^x = a^x \times b^x$.

Example:

1) Simplify. $(3x^5y^4)^2 =$

Use Exponent's rules: $(x^a)^b = x^{a \times b}$

$(3x^5y^4)^2 = (3)^2(x^5)^2(y^4)^2 = 9x^{5 \times 2}y^{4 \times 2} = 9x^{25}y^{16}$

2) Simplify. $\left(\frac{2x}{3x^2}\right)^2 =$

First cancel the common factor: $x \rightarrow \left(\frac{2x}{3x^2}\right)^2 = \left(\frac{2}{3x}\right)^2$

Use Exponent's rules: $\left(\frac{a}{b}\right)^c = \frac{a^c}{b^c}$

Then: $\left(\frac{2}{3x}\right)^2 = \frac{2^2}{(3x)^2} = \frac{4}{9x^2}$

✍ *Simplify.*

1) $(4x^3x^3)^2 =$

2) $(3x^3 \times 5x)^2 =$

3) $(10x^{11}y^3)^2 =$

4) $(9x^7 \quad ^5)^2 =$

5) $(4x^4y^6)^5 =$

6) $(3x \times 4y^3)^2 =$

7) $\left(\frac{5x}{x^2}\right)^2 =$

8) $\left(\frac{x^4y^4}{x^2y^2}\right)^3 =$

9) $\left(\frac{25x}{5x^6}\right)^2 =$

10) $\left(\frac{x^8}{x^6y^2}\right)^2 =$

11) $\left(\frac{xy^2}{x^3y^3}\right)^{-2} =$

12) $\left(\frac{2xy^4}{x^3}\right)^2 =$

Answers – Day 12

Multiplication Property of Exponents

1) $3x^5$
2) $2x^3$
3) $25x^8$
4) $4x^3y$
5) $3x^8y^2$
6) x^5y^7

7) $8x^5y^4$
8) $36x^5y^4$
9) $21x^6y^8$
10) $63x^3y^8$
11) $28x^4y^7$
12) $24x^7y^6$

Division Property of Exponents

1) 3
2) $\dfrac{1}{2x^2}$
3) $\dfrac{3}{2x^2}$
4) $\dfrac{6}{7^3}$
5) $\dfrac{4x^3}{3y^8}$
6) $\dfrac{5y^2}{x^5}$

7) $\dfrac{2x^3}{7}$
8) $\dfrac{4y^8}{x}$
9) $\dfrac{4}{5x^3y^9}$
10) $\dfrac{6}{5x^4}$
11) $\dfrac{16}{9x^4y}$
12) $\dfrac{1}{4}$

Powers of Products and Quotients

1) $16x^{12}$
2) $225x^8$
3) $100x^{22}y^6$
4) $81x^{14}y^{10}$
5) $1{,}024x^{20}y^{30}$
6) $144x^2y^6$
7) $\dfrac{25}{x^2}$

8) x^6y^6
9) $\dfrac{25}{x^{10}}$
10) $\dfrac{x^4}{y^4}$
11) x^4y^2
12) $\dfrac{4y^8}{x^4}$

Day 13:
Exponents and Roots

Math Topics that you'll learn today:

✓ Zero and Negative Exponents

✓ Negative Exponents and Negative Bases

✓ Scientific Notation

✓ Square Roots

Mathematics is an independent world created out of pure intelligence.

~ William Woods Worth

Zero and Negative Exponents

Step-by-step guide:

✓ A negative exponent simply means that the base is on the wrong side of the fraction line, so you need to flip the base to the other side. For instance, "x^{-2}" (pronounced as "ecks to the minus two") just means "x^2" but underneath, as in $\frac{1}{x^2}$.

Example:

1) Evaluate. $\left(\frac{4}{9}\right)^{-2} =$

Use Exponent's rules: $\frac{1}{b} = x^{-b} \rightarrow \left(\frac{4}{9}\right)^{-2} = \frac{1}{\left(\frac{4}{9}\right)^2} = \frac{1}{\frac{4^2}{9^2}}$

Now use fraction rule: $\frac{1}{\frac{b}{c}} = \frac{c}{b} \rightarrow \frac{1}{\frac{4^2}{9^2}} = \frac{9^2}{4^2} = \frac{81}{16}$

2) Evaluate. $\left(\frac{5}{6}\right)^{-3} =$

Use Exponent's rules: $\frac{1}{x^b} = x^{-b} \rightarrow \left(\frac{5}{6}\right)^{-3} = \frac{1}{\left(\frac{5}{6}\right)^3} = \frac{1}{\frac{5^3}{6^3}}$

Now use fraction rule: $\frac{1}{\frac{b}{c}} = \frac{c}{b} \rightarrow \frac{1}{\frac{5^3}{6^3}} = \frac{6^3}{5^3} = \frac{216}{125}$

✍ *Evaluate the following expressions.*

1) $2^{-3} =$

2) $3^{-3} =$

3) $7^{-3} =$

4) $6^{-3} =$

5) $8^{-3} =$

6) $9^{-2} =$

7) $10^{-3} =$

8) $10^{-9} =$

9) $\left(\frac{1}{2}\right)^{-1}$

10) $\left(\frac{1}{2}\right)^{-2} =$

11) $\left(\frac{1}{3}\right)^{-2} =$

12) $\left(\frac{2}{3}\right)^{-2} =$

Negative Exponents and Negative Bases

Step-by-step guide:

- ✓ Make the power positive. A negative exponent is the reciprocal of that number with a positive exponent.
- ✓ The parenthesis is important!
- ✓ 5^{-2} is not the same as $(-5)^{-2}$

$$(-5)^{-2} = -\frac{1}{5^2} \text{ and } (-5)^{-2} = +\frac{1}{5^2}$$

Example:

1) Simplify. $\left(\frac{3a}{2c}\right)^{-2} =$

Use Exponent's rules: $\frac{1}{x^b} = x^{-b} \rightarrow \left(\frac{3a}{2c}\right)^{-2} = \frac{1}{\left(\frac{3a}{2c}\right)^2} = \frac{1}{\frac{3^2 a^2}{2^2 c^2}}$

Now use fraction rule: $\frac{1}{\frac{b}{c}} = \frac{c}{b} \rightarrow \frac{1}{\frac{3^2 a^2}{2^2 c^2}} = \frac{2^2 c^2}{3^2 a^2}$

Then: $\frac{2^2 c^2}{3^2 a^2} = \frac{4c^2}{9a^2}$

2) Simplify. $\left(-\frac{5x}{3yz}\right)^{-3} =$

Use Exponent's rules: $\frac{1}{x^b} = x^{-b} \rightarrow \left(-\frac{5x}{3y}\right)^{-3} = \frac{1}{\left(-\frac{5x}{3yz}\right)^3} = \frac{1}{-\frac{5^3 x^3}{3^3 y^3 z^3}}$

Now use fraction rule: $\frac{1}{\frac{b}{c}} = \frac{c}{b} \rightarrow \frac{1}{-\frac{5^3 x^3}{3^3 y^3 z^3}} = -\frac{3^3 y^3 z^3}{5^3 x^3} = -\frac{27 y^3 z^3}{125 x^3}$

✎ *Simplify.*

1) $-5x^{-2}y^{-3} =$

2) $20x^{-4}y^{-1} =$

3) $14a^{-6}b^{-7} =$

4) $-12x^2 y^{-3} =$

5) $-\frac{25}{x^{-6}} =$

6) $\frac{7b}{-9 \ ^{-4}} =$

7) $\frac{7a}{a^{-3}b^{-1}} =$

8) $-\frac{5n^{-2}}{10p^{-3}} =$

9) $\frac{4a \ ^{-2}}{-3c^{-2}} =$

10) $\left(\frac{3a}{2c}\right)^{-2} =$

11) $\left(-\frac{5x}{3yz}\right)^{-3} =$

12) $\frac{4ab^{-2}}{-3c^{-2}} =$

13) $\left(-\frac{x^3}{x^4}\right)^{-2} =$

Scientific Notation

Step-by-step guide:

✓ It is used to write very big or very small numbers in decimal form.
✓ In scientific notation all numbers are written in the form of:

$$m \times 10^n$$

Decimal notation	Scientific notation
5	5×10^0
− 25,000	$- 2.5 \times 10^4$
0.5	5×10^{-1}
2,122.456	$2,122456 \times 10^3$

Example:

1) Write 0.00012 in scientific notation.

First, move the decimal point to the right so that you have a number that is between 1 and 10. Then: $N = 1.2$

Second, determine how many places the decimal moved in step 1 by the power of 10.
Then: $10^{-4} \rightarrow$ When the decimal moved to the right, the exponent is negative.
Then: $0.00012 = 1.2 \times 10^{-4}$

2) Write 8.3×10^{-5} in standard notation.

$10^{-5} \rightarrow$ When the decimal moved to the right, the exponent is negative.
Then: $8.3 \times 10^{-5} = 0.000083$

 **Write each number in scientific notation.**

1) $0.000325 =$

2) $0.00023 =$

3) $56,000,000 =$

4) $21,000 =$

 **Write each number in standard notation.**

5) $3 \times 10^{-1} =$

6) $5 \times 10^{-2} =$

7) $1.2 \times 10^3 =$

8) $2 \times 10^{-4} =$

Square Roots

Step-by-step guide:

- ✓ A square root of x is a number r whose square is: $r^2 = x$

    r is a square root of x.

Example:

1) Find the square root of $\sqrt{225}$.

First factor the number: $225 = 15^2$, Then: $\sqrt{225} = \sqrt{15^2}$

Now use radical rule: $\sqrt[n]{a^n} = a$

Then: $\sqrt{15^2} = 15$

2) Evaluate. $\sqrt{4} \times \sqrt{16} =$

First factor the numbers: $4 = 2^2$ and $16 = 4^2$

Then: $\sqrt{4} \times \sqrt{16} = \sqrt{2^2} \times \sqrt{4^2}$

Now use radical rule: $\sqrt[n]{a^n} = a$, Then: $\sqrt{2^2} \times \sqrt{4^2} = 2 \times 4 = 8$

✎ *Evaluate.*

1) $\sqrt{4} \times \sqrt{9} = $ _____

2) $\sqrt{25} \times \sqrt{64} = $ _____

3) $\sqrt{2} \times \sqrt{8} = $ _____

4) $\sqrt{6} \times \sqrt{6} = $ _____

5) $\sqrt{5} \times \sqrt{5} = $ _____

6) $\sqrt{8} \times \sqrt{8} = $ _____

7) $\sqrt{2} + \sqrt{2} = $ _____

8) $\sqrt{8} + \sqrt{8} = $ _____

9) $4\sqrt{5} - 2\sqrt{5} = $ _____

10) $3\sqrt{3} \times 2\sqrt{3} = $ _____

11) $8\sqrt{2} \times 2\sqrt{2} = $ _____

12) $6\sqrt{3} - \sqrt{12} = $ _____

Answers – Day 13

Zero and Negative Exponents

1) $\dfrac{1}{8}$

2) $\dfrac{1}{27}$

3) $\dfrac{1}{343}$

4) $\dfrac{1}{216}$

5) $\dfrac{1}{512}$

6) $\dfrac{1}{81}$

7) $\dfrac{1}{1,000}$

8) $\dfrac{1}{1,000,000,000}$

9) 2

10) 4

11) 9

12) $\dfrac{9}{4}$

Negative Exponents and Negative Bases

1) $-\dfrac{5}{x^2}\,^3$

2) $\dfrac{20}{x^4 y}$

3) $\dfrac{14}{a^6 b^7}$

4) $-\dfrac{12x^2}{y^3}$

5) $-25x^6$

6) $-\dfrac{7bc^4}{9}$

7) $7a^4 b^2$

8) $-\dfrac{p^3}{2n^2}$

9) $-\dfrac{4ac^2}{3b^2}$

10) $\dfrac{4c^2}{9a^2}$

11) $-\dfrac{27\,^3 z^3}{125x^3}$

12) $-\dfrac{4ac^2}{3b^2}$

13) $\;^2$

Scientific Notation

1) 3.25×10^{-4}
2) 2.3×10^{-4}
3) 5.6×10^7

4) 2.1×10^4
5) 0.3
6) 0.05

7) $1,200$
8) 0.0002

Square Roots

1) 6
2) 40
3) 4
4) 6
5) 5

6) 8
7) $2\sqrt{2}$
8) $2\sqrt{8}$
9) $2\sqrt{5}$

10) 18
11) 32
12) $4\sqrt{3}$

Day 14:
Expressions and Variables

Math Topics that you'll learn today:

✓ Simplifying Variable Expressions

✓ Simplifying Polynomial Expressions

✓ Translate Phrases into an Algebraic Statement

Mathematics is, as it were, a sensuous logic, and relates to philosophy as do the arts, music, and plastic art to poetry. – K.

Shegel

Simplifying Variable Expressions

Step-by-step guide:

- ✓ In algebra, a variable is a letter used to stand for a number. The most common letters are: $x, y, z, a, b, c, m, and\ n$.
- ✓ algebraic expression is an expression contains integers, variables, and the math operations such as addition, subtraction, multiplication, division, etc.
- ✓ In an expression, we can combine "like" terms. (values with same variable and same power)

Examples:

1) Simplify this expression. $(10x + 2x + 3) =?$
   Combine like terms. Then: $(10x + 2x + 3) = 12x + 3$ (remember you cannot combine variables and numbers.

2) Simplify this expression. $12 - 3x^2 + 9x + 5x^2 =?$
   Combine "like" terms: $-3x^2 + 5x^2 = 2x^2$

   Then: $12 - 3x^2 + 9x + 5x^2 = 12 + 2x^2 + 9x$. Write in standard form (biggest powers first): $2x^2 + 9x + 12$

✍ *Simplify each expression.*

1) $(2x + x + 3 + 24) =$

2) $(-28x - 20x + 24) =$

3) $7x + 3 - 3x =$

4) $-2 - x^2 - 6x^2 =$

5) $3 + 10x^2 + 2 =$

6) $8x^2 + 6x + 7x^2 =$

7) $5x^2 - 12x^2 + 8x =$

8) $2x^2 - 2x - x =$

9) $4x + (12 - 30x) =$

10) $10x + (80x - 48) =$

11) $(-18x - 54) - 5 =$

12) $2x^2 + (-8x) =$

Simplifying Polynomial Expressions

Step-by-step guide:

✓ In mathematics, a polynomial is an expression consisting of variables and coefficients that involves only the operations of addition, subtraction, multiplication, and non-negative integer exponents of variables.

$$P(x) = a_n x^n + a_{n-1} x^{n-1} + \ldots + a_2 x^2 + a_1 x + a_0$$

Examples:

1) Simplify this Polynomial Expressions. $4x^2 - 5x^3 + 15x^4 - 12x^3 =$
   Combine "like" terms: $-5x^3 - 12x^3 = -17x^3$
   Then: $4x^2 - 5x^3 + 15x^4 - 12x^3 = 4x^2 - 17x^3 + 15x^4$
   Then write in standard form: $4x^2 - 17x^3 + 15x^4 = 15x^4 - 17x^3 + 4x^2$

2) Simplify this expression. $(2x^2 - x^4) - (4x^4 - x^2) =$
   First use distributive property: → multiply $(-)$ into $(4x^4 - x^2)$
   $(2x^2 - x^4) - (4x^4 - x^2) = 2x^2 - x^4 - 4x^4 + x^2$
   Then combine "like" terms: $2x^2 - x^4 - 4x^4 + x^2 = 3x^2 - 5x^4$
   And write in standard form: $3x^2 - 5x^4 = -5x^4 + 3x^2$

✎ *Simplify each polynomial.*

1) $(2x^3 + 5x^2) - (12x + 2x^2) =$ _____

2) $(2x^5 + 2x^3) - (7x^3 + 6x^2) =$ _____

3) $(12x^4 + 4x^2) - (2x^2 - 6x^4) =$ _____

4) $14x - 3x^2 - 2(6x^2 + 6x^3) =$ _____

5) $(5x^3 - 3) + 5(2x^2 - 3x^3) =$ _____

6) $(4x^3 - 2x) - 2(4x^3 - 2x^4) =$ _____

7) $2(4x - 3x^3) - 3(3x^3 + 4x^2) =$ _____

8) $(2x^2 - 2x) - (2x^3 + 5x^2) =$ _____

Translate Phrases into an Algebraic Statement

Step-by-step guide:

Translating key words and phrases into algebraic expressions:

- ✓ Addition: plus, more than, the sum of, etc.
- ✓ Subtraction: minus, less than, decreased, etc.
- ✓ Multiplication: times, product, multiplied, etc.
- ✓ Division: quotient, divided, ratio, etc.

Examples:

Write an algebraic expression for each phrase.

1) Eight more than a number is 20.
   More than mean plus a number $= x$
   Then: $8 + x = 20$

2) 5 times the sum of 8 and x.
   Sum of 8 and x: $8 + x$. Times means multiplication. Then: $5 \times (8 + x)$

✎ *Write an algebraic expression for each phrase.*

1) 4 multiplied by x. _____

2) Subtract 8 from y. _____

3) 6 divided by x. _____

4) 12 decreased by y. _____

5) Add y to 9. _____

6) The square of 5. _____

7) x raised to the fourth power. _____

8) The sum of nine and a number. _____

9) The difference between sixty–four and y. _____

10) The quotient of twelve and a number. _____

11) The quotient of the square of x and 7. _____

12) The difference between x and 8 is 22. _____

Answers – Day 14

Simplifying Variable Expressions

1) $3x + 27$
2) $-48x + 24$
3) $4x + 3$
4) $-7x^2 - 2$
5) $10x^2 + 5$
6) $15x^2 + 6x$

7) $-7x^2 + 8x$
8) $2x^2 - 3x$
9) $-26x + 12$
10) $90x - 48$
11) $-18x - 59$
12) $2x^2 - 8x$

Simplifying Polynomial Expressions

1) $2x^3 + 3x^2 - 12x$
2) $2x^5 - 5x^3 - 6x^2$
3) $18x^4 + 2x^2$
4) $-12x^3 - 15x^2 + 14x$

5) $-10x^3 + 10x^2 - 3$
6) $4x^4 - 4x^3 - 2$
7) $-15x^3 - 12x^2 + 8x$
8) $-2x^3 - 3x^2 - 2x$

Translate Phrases into an Algebraic Statement

1) $4x$
2) $y - 8$
3) $\frac{6}{x}$
4) $12 - y$
5) $y + 9$
6) 5^2
7) x^4

8) $9 + x$
9) $64 - y$
10) $\frac{12}{x}$
11) $\frac{x^2}{7}$
12) $x - 8 = 22$

Day 15:
Evaluating Variables

Math Topics that you'll learn today:

✓ The Distributive Property

✓ Evaluating One Variable

✓ Evaluating Two Variables

✓ Combining like Terms

Mathematics is on the artistic side a creation of new rhythms, orders, designs, harmonies, and on the knowledge side, is a systematic study of various rhythms, orders. – William L. Schaaf

The Distributive Property

Step-by-step guide:

✓ Distributive Property:
$$a(b + c) = ab + ac$$

Examples:

1) Simply. $(5x - 3)(-5) =$

   Use Distributive Property formula: $a(b + c) = ab + ac$
   $(5x - 3)(-5) = -25x + 15$

2) Simply $(-8)(2x - 8) =$

   Use Distributive Property formula: $a(b + c) = ab + ac$
   $(-8)(2x - 8) = -16x + 64$

✎ *Use the distributive property to simply each expression.*

1) $2(2 + 3x) =$

2) $3(5 + 5x) =$

3) $4(3x - 8) =$

4) $(6x - 2)(-2) =$

5) $(-3)(x + 2) =$

6) $(2 + 2x)5 =$

7) $(-4)(4 - 2x) =$

8) $-(-2 - 5x) =$

9) $(-6x + 2)(-1) =$

10) $(-5)(x - 2) =$

11) $-(7 - 3x) =$

12) $8(8 + 2x) =$

Evaluating One Variable

Step-by-step guide:

- ✓ To evaluate one variable expression, find the variable and substitute a number for that variable.
- ✓ Perform the arithmetic operations.

Examples:

1) Solve this expression. $12 - 2x$, $x = -1$

   First substitute -1 for x, then:

   $12 - 2x = 12 - 2(-1) = 12 + 2 = 14$

2) Solve this expression. $-8 + 5x$, $x = 3$

   First substitute 3 for x, then:

   $-8 + 5x = -8 + 5(3) = -8 + 15 = 7$

🖎 *Evaluate each expression using the value given.*

1) $5 + x$, $x = 2$

2) $x - 2, x = 4$

3) $8x + 1, x = 9$

4) $x - 12, x = -1$

5) $9 - x$, $x = 3$

6) $x + 2, x = 5$

7) $3x + 7, x = 6$

8) $x + (-5), x = -2$

9) $3x + 6, x = 4$

10) $4x + 6, x = -1$

11) $10 + 2x - 6, x = 3$

12) $10 - 3x, x = 8$

Evaluating Two Variables

Step-by-step guide:

✓ To evaluate an algebraic expression, substitute a number for each variable and perform the arithmetic operations.

Examples:

1) Solve this expression. $-3x + 5y$, $x = 2, y = -1$

First substitute 2 for x, and -1 for y, then:

$-3x + 5y = -3(2) + 5(-1) = -6 - 5 = -11$

2) Solve this expression. $2(a - 2b), a = -1, b = 3$

First substitute -1 for a, and 3 for b, then:

$2(a - 2b) = 2a - 4b = 2(-1) - 4(3) = -2 - 12 = -14$

✍ *Evaluate each expression using the values given.*

1) $2x + 4y$,

$x = 3, y = 2$

2) $8x + 5y$,

$x = 1, y = 5$

3) $-2a + 4b$,

$a = 6, b = 3$

4) $4x + 7 - 2y$,

$x = 7, y = 6$

5) $5z + 12 - 4k$,

$z = 5, k = 2$

6) $2(-x - 2y)$,

$x = 6, y = 9$

7) $18a + 2b$,

$a = 2, b = 8$

8) $4x \div 3y$,

$x = 3, y = 2$

9) $2x + 15 + 4y$,

$x = -2, y = 4$

10) $4a - (15 - b)$,

$a = 4, b = 6$

11) $5z + 19 + 8k$,

$z = -5, k = 4$

12) $xy + 12 + 5x$,

$x = 7, y = 2$

Combining like Terms

Step-by-step guide:

- ✓ Terms are separated by "+" and "-" signs.
- ✓ Like terms are terms with same variables and same powers.
- ✓ Be sure to use the "+" or "-" that is in front of the coefficient.

Examples:

1) Simplify this expression. $(-5)(8x - 6) =$

Use Distributive Property formula: $a(b + c) = a + ac$
$(-5)(8x - 6) = -40x + 30$

2) Simplify this expression. $(-3)(2x - 2) + 6 =$

First use Distributive Property formula: $a(b + c) = ab + ac$
$(-3)(2x - 2) + 6 = -6x + 6 + 6$

And Combining like Terms:

$-6x + 6 + 6 = -6x + 12$

✎ *Simplify each expression.*

1) $2x + x + 2 =$

2) $2(5x - 3) =$

3) $7x - 2x + 8 =$

4) $(-4)(3x - 5) =$

5) $9x - 7x - 5 =$

6) $16x - 5 + 8x =$

7) $5 - (5x + 6) =$

8) $-12x + 7 - 10x =$

9) $7x - 11 - 2x + 2 =$

10) $12x + 4x - 21 =$

11) $5 + 2x - 8 =$

12) $(-2x + 6)^2 =$

Answers – Day 15

The Distributive Property

1) $6x + 4$
2) $15x + 15$
3) $12x - 32$
4) $-12x + 4$
5) $-3x - 6$
6) $10x + 10$

7) $8x - 16$
8) $5x + 2$
9) $6x - 2$
10) $-5x + 10$
11) $3x - 7$
12) $16x + 64$

Evaluating One Variable

1) 7
2) 2
3) 73
4) -13
5) 6
6) 7

7) 25
8) -7
9) 18
10) 2
11) 10
12) -14

Evaluating Two Variables

1) 14
2) 33
3) 0
4) 23
5) 29
6) -48

7) 52
8) 2
9) 27
10) 7
11) 26
12) 61

Combining like Terms

1) $3x + 2$
2) $10x - 6$
3) $5x + 8$
4) $-12x + 20$
5) $2x - 5$
6) $24x - 5$

7) $-5x - 1$
8) $-22x + 7$
9) $5x - 9$
10) $16x - 21$
11) $2x - 3$
12) $4x^2 - 24x + 36$

Day 16:
Equations and Inequalities

Math Topics that you'll learn today:

- ✓ One–Step Equations

- ✓ Multi–Step Equations

- ✓ Graphing Single–Variable Inequalities

"Life is a math equation. In order to gain the most, you have to know how to convert negatives into positives."

- Anonymous

One–Step Equations

Step-by-step guide:

✓ The values of two expressions on both sides of an equation are equal. $ax + b = c$

✓ You only need to perform one Math operation in order to solve the one-step equations.

✓ To solve one-step equation, find the inverse (opposite) operation is being performed.

✓ The inverse operations are:
  - Addition and subtraction
  - Multiplication and division

Examples:

1) Solve this equation. $x + 24 = 0$, $x = ?$
   Here, the operation is addition and its inverse operation is subtraction. To solve this equation, subtract 24 from both sides of the equation: $x + 24 - 24 = 0 - 24$
   Then simplify: $x + 24 - 24 = 0 - 24 \rightarrow x = -24$

2) Solve this equation. $3x = 15$, $x = ?$
   Here, the operation is multiplication (variable x is multiplied by 3) and its inverse operation is division. To solve this equation, divide both sides of equation by 3:
   $$3x = 15 \rightarrow 3x \div 3 = 15 \div 3 \rightarrow x = 5$$

✎ *Solve each equation.*

1) $16 = -4 + x, x = $ ____

2) $x - 4 = -25, x = $ ____

3) $x + 12 = -9, x = $ ____

4) $14 = 18 - x, x = $ ____

5) $2 + x = -14, x = $ ____

6) $x - 5 = 15, x = $ ____

7) $25 = x - 5, x = $ ____

8) $x - 3 = -12, x = $ ____

9) $x - 12 = 12, x = $ ____

10) $x - 12 = -25, x = $ ____

11) $x - 13 = 32, x = $ ____

12) $-55 = x - 18, x = $ ____

Multi–Step Equations

Step-by-step guide:

✓ Combine "like" terms on one side.
✓ Bring variables to one side by adding or subtracting.
✓ Simplify using the inverse of addition or subtraction.
✓ Simplify further by using the inverse of multiplication or division.

Examples:

1) Solve this equation. $-(2 - x) = 5$

First use Distributive Property: $-(2 - x) = -2 + x$

Now solve by adding 2 to both sides of the equation. $-2 + x = 5 \rightarrow -2 + x + 2 = 5 + 2$

Now simplify: $-2 + x + 2 = 5 + 2 \rightarrow x = 7$

2) Solve this equation. $4x + 10 = 25 - x$

First bring variables to one side by adding x to both sides.

$4x + 10 + x = 25 - x + x \rightarrow 5x + 10 = 25$. Now, subtract 10 from both sides:

$5x + 10 - 10 = 25 - 10 \rightarrow 5x = 15$

Now, divide both sides by 5: $5x = 15 \rightarrow 5x \div 5 = \frac{15}{5} \rightarrow x = 3$

✍ *Solve each equation.*

1) $-3(2 + x) = 3$

2) $-2(4 + x) = 4$

3) $20 = -(x - 8)$

4) $2(2 - 2x) = 20$

5) $-12 = -(2x + 8)$

6) $5(2 + x) = 5$

7) $2(x - 14) = 4$

8) $-28 = 2x + 12x$

9) $3x + 15 = -x - 5$

10) $2(3 + 2x) = -18$

11) $12 - 2x = -8 - x$

12) $10 - 3x = 14 + x$

Graphing Single–Variable Inequalities

Step-by-step guide:

- ✓ Inequality is similar to equations and uses symbols for "less than" (<) and "greater than" (>).
- ✓ To solve inequalities, we need to isolate the variable. (like in equations)
- ✓ To graph an inequality, find the value of the inequality on the number line.
- ✓ For less than or greater than draw open circle on the value of the variable.
- ✓ If there is an equal sign too, then use filled circle.
- ✓ Draw a line to the right or to the left for greater or less than.

Examples:

1) Draw a graph for $x > 2$

Since, the variable is greater than 2, then we need to find 2 and draw an open circle above it. Then, draw a line to the right.

Graph this inequality. $x < 5$

✎ *Draw a graph for each inequality.*

1) $x > -1$

2) $x < 3$

3) $x < -5$

4) $x > -2$

5) $x < 0$

Answers – Day 16

One–Step Equations

1) 20
2) −21
3) −21
4) 4
5) −16
6) 20

7) 30
8) −9
9) 24
10) −13
11) 45
12) −37

Multi–Step Equations

1) −3
2) −6
3) −12
4) −4
5) 2
6) −1

7) 16
8) −2
9) −5
10) −6
11) 20
12) −1

Graphing Single–Variable Inequalities

1)

2)

3)

4)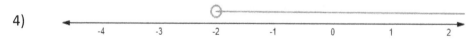

5)

Day 17:
Solving Inequalities

Math Topics that you'll learn today:

- ✓ One–Step Inequalities

- ✓ Multi–Step Inequalities

Go down deep enough into anything and you will find mathematics." ~ Dean Schlicter

One–Step Inequalities

Step-by-step guide:

- ✓ Similar to equations, first isolate the variable by using inverse operation.
- ✓ For dividing or multiplying both sides by negative numbers, flip the direction of the inequality sign.

Examples:

1) Solve and graph the inequality. $x + 2 \geq 3$.

Subtract 2 from both sides. $x + 2 \geq 3 \rightarrow x + 2 - 2 \geq 3 - 2$, then: $x \geq 1$

2) Solve this inequality. $x - 1 \leq 2$

Add 1 to both sides. $x - 1 \leq 2 \rightarrow x - 1 + 1 \leq 2 + 1$, then: $x \leq 3$

✎ *Solve each inequality and graph it.*

1) $2x \geq 12$

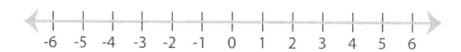

2) $4 + x \leq 5$

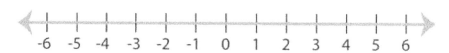

3) $x + 3 \leq -3$

4) $4x \geq 16$

5) $9x \leq 18$

Multi–Step Inequalities

Step-by-step guide:

- ✓ Isolate the variable.
- ✓ Simplify using the inverse of addition or subtraction.
- ✓ Simplify further by using the inverse of multiplication or division.

Examples:

1) Solve this inequality. $2x - 2 \leq 6$

First add 2 to both sides: $2x - 2 + 2 \leq 6 + 2 \rightarrow 2x \leq 8$

Now, divide both sides by 2: $2x \leq 8 \rightarrow x \leq 4$

2) Solve this inequality. $2x - 4 \leq 8$

First add 4 to both sides: $2x - 4 + 4 \leq 8 + 4$

Then simplify: $2x - 4 + 4 \leq 8 + 4 \rightarrow 2x \leq 12$

Now divide both sides by 2: $\frac{2x}{2} \leq \frac{12}{2} \rightarrow x \leq 6$

✍ *Solve each inequality.*

1) $2x - 8 \leq 6$

2) $8x - 2 \leq 14$

3) $-5 + 3x \leq 10$

4) $2(x - 3) \leq 6$

5) $7x - 5 \leq 9$

6) $4x - 21 < 19$

7) $2x - 3 < 21$

8) $17 - 3x \geq -13$

9) $9 + 4x < 21$

10) $3 + 2x \geq 19$

11) $6 + 2x < 32$

12) $4x - 1 < 7$

Answers – Day 17

One–Step Inequalities

1)
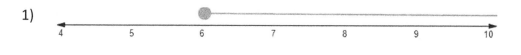

2)

3)

4)

5)

Multi–Step inequalities

1) $x \leq 7$
2) $x \leq 2$
3) $x \leq 5$
4) $x \leq 6$
5) $x \leq 2$
6) $x < 10$
7) $x < 12$
8) $x \geq 10 \ x \leq 10$
9) $x < 3$
10) $x \geq 8$
11) $x < 13$
12) $x < 2$

Day 18:
Lines and Slope

Math Topics that you'll learn today:

✓ Finding Slope

✓ Graphing Lines Using Slope–Intercept Form

✓ Graphing Lines Using Standard Form

"Nature is written in mathematical language." – Galileo Galilei

Finding Slope

Step-by-step guide:

- ✓ The slope of a line represents the direction of a line on the coordinate plane.
- ✓ A coordinate plane contains two perpendicular number lines. The horizontal line is x and the vertical line is y. The point at which the two axes intersect is called the origin. An ordered pair (x, y) shows the location of a point.
- ✓ A line on coordinate plane can be drawn by connecting two points.
- ✓ To find the slope of a line, we need two points.
- ✓ The slope of a line with two points A (x_1, y_1) and B (x_2, y_2) can be found by using this formula: $\frac{y_2 - y_1}{x_2 - x_1} = \frac{rise}{run}$

Examples:

1) Find the slope of the line through these two points: $(2, -10)$ *and* $(3, 6)$.

   Slope $= \frac{y_2 - y_1}{x_2 - x_1}$. Let (x_1, y_1) be $(2, -10)$ and (x_2, y_2) be $(3, 6)$. Then: slope $= \frac{y_2 - y_1}{x_2 - x_1} = \frac{6 - (-10)}{3 - 2} = \frac{6 + 10}{1} = \frac{16}{1} = 16$

2) Find the slope of the line containing two points $(8, 3)$ and $(-4, 9)$.

   Slope $= \frac{y_2 - y_1}{x_2 - x_1} \rightarrow (x_1, y_1) = (8, 3)$ and $(x_2, y_2) = (-4, 9)$. Then: slope $= \frac{y_2 - y_1}{x_2 - x_1} = \frac{9 - 3}{-4 - 8} = \frac{6}{-12} = \frac{1}{-2} = -\frac{1}{2}$

✍ *Find the slope of the line through each pair of points.*

1) $(1, 1), (2, 3)$

2) $(-1, 2), (0, 3)$

3) $(3, -1), (2, 3)$

4) $(-2, -1), (0, 5)$

5) $(5, 1), (2, 4)$

6) $(-3, 1), (-2, 4)$

7) $(6, 2), (7, 4)$

8) $(6, -5), (3, 4)$

9) $(12, -9), (11, -8)$

10) $(7, 4), (5, -2)$

11) $(1, 1), (3, 5)$

12) $(7, -12), (5, 10)$

Graphing Lines Using Slope–Intercept Form

Step-by-step guide:

✓ Slope-intercept form of a line: given the slope m and the y-intercept (the intersection of the line and y-axis) b, then the equation of the line is:
$$y = mx + b$$

Example: *Sketch the graph of* $y = 8x - 3$.

To graph this line, we need to find two points. When x is zero the value of y is -3. And when y is zero the value of x is 3/8. $x = 0 \rightarrow y = 8(0) - 3 = -3, y = 0 \rightarrow 0 = 8x - 3 \rightarrow x = \frac{3}{8}$

Now, we have two points: $(0, -3)$ and $(\frac{3}{8}, 0)$. Find the points and graph the line. Remember that the slope of the line is 8.

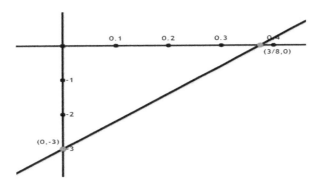

✐ ***Sketch the graph of each line.***

1) $y = \frac{1}{2}x - 4$

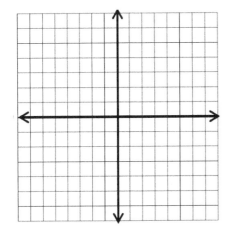

2) $y = 2x$

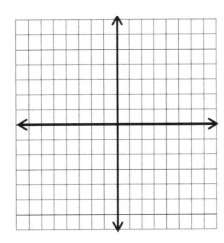

Graphing Lines Using Standard Form

Step-by-step guide:

- ✓ Find the x −intercept of the line by putting zero for y.
- ✓ Find the y −intercept of the line by putting zero for the x.
- ✓ Connect these two points.

Example:

Sketch the graph of $x - y = -5$.

First isolate y for x: $x - y = -5 \rightarrow y = x + 5$

Find the x-intercept of the line by putting zero for y.

$y = x + 5 \rightarrow x + 5 = 0 \rightarrow x = -5$

Find the y-intercept of the line by putting zero for the x.

$y = 0 + 5 \rightarrow y = 5$

Then: x-intercept: $(-5,0)$ and y-intercept: $(0,5)$

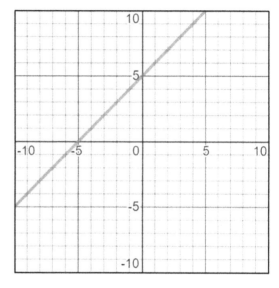

✍ ***Sketch the graph of each line.***

1) $y = 3x - 2$　　　　2) $y = -x + 1$　　　　3) $x + y = 4$

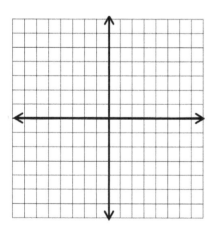　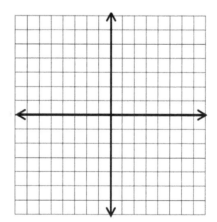　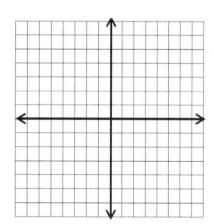

100

Answers – Day 18

Finding Slope

1) 2
2) 1
3) −4
4) 3
5) −1
6) 3

7) 2
8) −3
9) −1
10) 3
11) 2
12) −11

Graphing Lines Using Slope–Intercept Form

1)

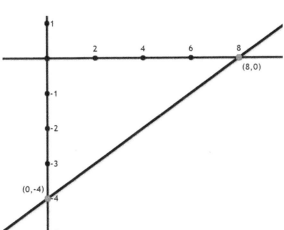

2)

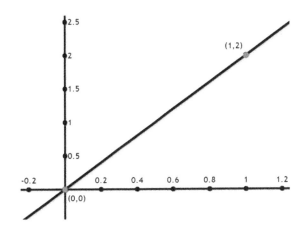

Graphing Lines Using Standard Form

1) $y = 3x - 2$

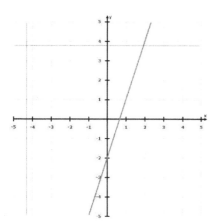

2) $y = -x + 1$

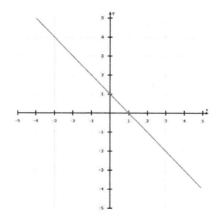

3) $x + y = 4$

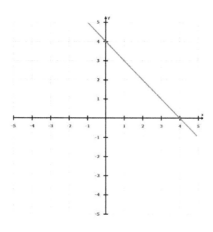

Day 19:
Linear Equations and Inequalities

Math Topics that you'll learn today:

- ✓ Writing Linear Equations

- ✓ Graphing Linear Inequalities

- ✓ Finding Midpoint

- ✓ Finding Distance of Two Points

Mathematics is a game played according to certain rules with meaningless marks on paper. ~ David Hilbert

Writing Linear Equations

Step-by-step guide:

- ✓ The equation of a line: $y = mx + b$
- ✓ Identify the slope.
- ✓ Find the y-intercept. This can be done by substituting the slope and the coordinates of a point (x, y) on the line.

Example:

1) What is the equation of the line that passes through $(2, -2)$ and has a slope of 7?

The general slope-intercept form of the equation of a line is $y = mx + b$, where m is the slope and b is the y-intercept.

By substitution of the given point and given slope, we have: $-2 = (2)(7) + b$

So, $b = -2 - 14 = -16$, and the required equation is $y = 2x - 16$.

2) Write the equation of the line through $(2, 1)$ and $(-1, 4)$.

$Slop = \frac{y_2 - y_1}{x_2 - x_1} = \frac{4 - 1}{-1 - 2} = \frac{3}{-3} = -1 \rightarrow m = -1$

To find the value of b, you can use either points. The answer will be the same: $y = -x + b$

$(2, 1) \rightarrow 1 = -2 + b \rightarrow b = 3$

$(-1, 4) \rightarrow 4 = -(-1) + b \rightarrow b = 3$

The equation of the line is: $y = -x + 3$

✎ ***Write the equation of the line through the given points.***

1) through: $(1, -2), (2, 3)$

2) through: $(-2, 1), (1, 4)$

3) through: $(-2, 1), (0, 5)$

4) through: $(5, 4), (2, 1)$

5) through: $(-4, 9), (3, 2)$

6) through: $(8, 3), (7, 2)$

7) through: $(7, -2), (5, 2)$

8) through: $(-3, 9), (5, -7)$

Graphing Linear Inequalities

Step-by-step guide:

- ✓ First, graph the "equals" line.
- ✓ Choose a testing point. (it can be any point on both sides of the line.)
- ✓ Put the value of (x, y) of that point in the inequality. If that works, that part of the line is the solution. If the values don't work, then the other part of the line is the solution.

Example:

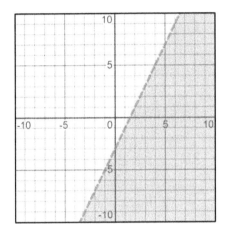

Sketch the graph of $y < 2x - 3$. First, graph the line:

$y = 2x - 3$. The slope is 2 and y-intercept is -3. Then, choose a testing point. The easiest point to test is the origin: $(0, 0)$

$$(0,0) \rightarrow y < 2x - 3 \rightarrow 0 < 2(0) - 3 \rightarrow 0 < -3$$

0 is not less than -3. So, the other part of the line (on the right side) is the solution.

✎ *Sketch the graph of each linear inequality.*

1) $y > 3x - 1$ 2) $y < -x + 4$ 3) $y \leq -5x + 8$

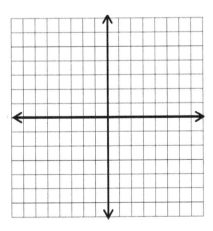 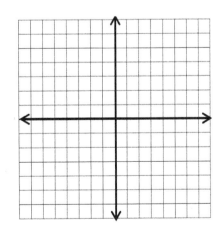 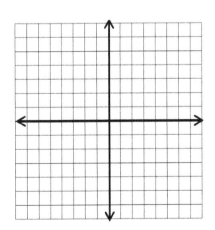

Finding Midpoint

Step-by-step guide:

- ✓ The middle of a line segment is its midpoint.
- ✓ The Midpoint of two endpoints A (x_1, y_1) and B (x_2, y_2) can be found using this formula: M $(\frac{x_1+x_2}{2}, \frac{y_1+y_2}{2})$

Example:

1) Find the midpoint of the line segment with the given endpoints. $(4, -5), (0, 9)$

Midpoint $= (\frac{x_1+x_2}{2}, \frac{y_1+y_2}{2}) \rightarrow (x_1, y_1) = (4, -5)$ and $(x_2, y_2) = (0, 9)$

Midpoint $= (\frac{4+0}{2}, \frac{-5+9}{2}) \rightarrow (\frac{4}{2}, \frac{4}{2}) \rightarrow M(2, 2)$

2) Find the midpoint of the line segment with the given endpoints. $(6, 7), (4, -5)$

Midpoint $= (\frac{x_1+x_2}{2}, \frac{y_1+y_2}{2}) \rightarrow (x_1, y_1) = (6, 7)$ and $(x_2, y_2) = (4, -5)$

Midpoint $= (\frac{6+4}{2}, \frac{7-5}{2}) \rightarrow (\frac{10}{2}, \frac{2}{2}) \rightarrow (5, 1)$

✎ *Find the midpoint of the line segment with the given endpoints.*

1) $(-2, -2), (0, 2)$

2) $(5, 1), (-2, 4)$

3) $(4, -1), (0, 3)$

4) $(-3, 5), (-1, 3)$

5) $(3, -2), (7, -6)$

6) $(-4, -3), (2, -7)$

7) $(5, 0), (-5, 8)$

8) $(-6, 4), (-2, 0)$

9) $(-3, 4), (9, -6)$

10) $(2, 8), (6, -2)$

11) $(4, 7), (-6, 5)$

12) $(9, 3), (-1, -7)$

Finding Distance of Two Points

Step-by-step guide:

✓ Distance of two points A (x_1, y_1) and B (x_2, y_2): $d = \sqrt{(x_1 - x_2)^2 + (y_1 - y_2)^2}$

Example:

1) Find the distance between of $(0, 8), (-4, 5)$.

Use distance of two points formula: $d = \sqrt{(x_1 - x_2)^2 + (y_1 - y_2)^2}$

$(x_1, y_1) = (0, 8)$ and $(x_2, y_2) = (-4, 5)$. Then: $d = \sqrt{(x_1 - x_2)^2 + (y_1 - y_2)^2} \rightarrow$

$d = \sqrt{(0 - (-4))^2 + (8 - 5)^2} = \sqrt{(4)^2 + (3)^2} = \sqrt{16 + 9} = \sqrt{25} = 5 \rightarrow d = 5$

2) Find the distance of two points $(4, 2)$ and $(-5, -10)$.

Use distance of two points formula: $d = \sqrt{(x_1 - x_2)^2 + (y_1 - y_2)^2}$

$(x_1, y_1) = (4, 2)$, and $(x_2, y_2) = (-5, -10)$

Then: $d = \sqrt{(x_1 - x_2)^2 + (y_1 - y_2)^2} \rightarrow d = \sqrt{(4 - (-5))^2 + (2 - (-10))^2} =$

$\sqrt{(9)^2 + (12)^2} = \sqrt{81 + 144} = \sqrt{225} = 15$. Then: $d = 15$

✍ *Find the distance between each pair of points.*

1) $(2, 1), (-1, -3)$

2) $(-2, -1), (2, 2)$

3) $(-1, 0), (5, 8)$

4) $(-4, -1), (1, 11)$

5) $(3, -2), (-6, -14)$

6) $(-6, 0), (-2, 3)$

7) $(3, 2), (11, 17)$

8) $(-6, -10), (6, -1)$

9) $(5, 9), (-11, -3)$

10) $(9, -3), (3, -11)$

11) $(2, 0), (12, 24)$

12) $(8, 4), (3, -8)$

Answers – Day 19

Writing Linear Equations

1) $y = 5x - 7$

2) $y = x + 3$

3) $y = 2x + 5$

4) $y = x - 1$

5) $y = -x + 5$

6) $y = x - 5$

7) $y = -2x + 12$

8) $y = -2x + 3$

Graphing Linear Inequalities

1) $y > 3x - 1$

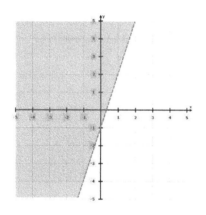

2) $y < -x + 4$

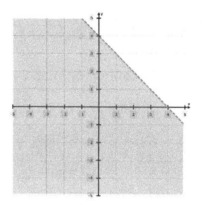

3) $y \leq -5x + 8$

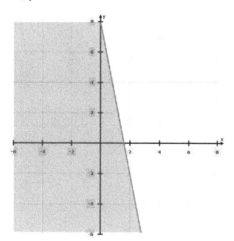

Finding Midpoint

1) $(-1, 0)$
2) $(1.5, 2.5)$
3) $(2, 1)$
4) $(-2, 4)$

5) $(5, -4)$
6) $(-1, -5)$
7) $(0, 4)$
8) $(-4, 2)$

9) $(3, -1)$
10) $(4, 3)$
11) $(-1, 6)$
12) $(4, -2)$

Finding Distance of Two Points

1) 5
2) 5
3) 10
4) 13

5) 15
6) 5
7) 17
8) 15

9) 20
10) 10
11) 26
12) 13

Day 20:
Polynomials

Math Topics that you'll learn today:

✓ Writing Polynomials in Standard Form

✓ Simplifying Polynomials

✓ Adding and Subtracting Polynomials

Mathematics is the supreme judge; from its decisions there is no appeal. - Tobias Dantzig

Writing Polynomials in Standard Form

Step-by-step guide:

✓ A polynomial function $f(x)$ of degree n is of the form
$$f(x) = a_n x^n + a_{n-1} x_{n-1} + \cdots + a_1 x + a_0$$

✓ The first term is the one with the biggest power!

Example:

1) Write this polynomial in standard form. $-12 + 3x^2 - 6x^4 =$

The first term is the one with the biggest power: $-12 + 3x^2 - 6x^4 = -6x^4 + 3x^2 - 12$

2) Write this polynomial in standard form. $5x^2 - 9x^5 + 8x^3 - 11 =$

The first term is the one with the biggest power: $5x^2 - 9x^5 + 8x^3 - 11 =$
$-9x^5 + 8x^3 + 5x^2 - 11$

✎ *Write each polynomial in standard form.*

1) $9x - 7x =$

2) $-3 + 16x - 16x =$

3) $3x^2 - 5x^3 =$

4) $3 + 4x^3 - 3 =$

5) $2x^2 + 1x - 6x^3 =$

6) $-x^2 + 2x^3 =$

7) $2x + 4x^3 - 2x^2 =$

8) $-2x^2 + 4x - 6x^3 =$

9) $2x^2 + 2 - 5x =$

10) $12 - 7x + 9x^4 =$

11) $5x^2 + 13x - 2x^3 =$

12) $10 + 6x^2 - x^3 =$

Simplifying Polynomials

Step-by-step guide:

   ✓ Find "like" terms. (they have same variables with same power).

   ✓ Use "FOIL". (First-Out-In-Last) for binomials:

$$(x + a)(x + b) = x^2 + (b + a)x + ab$$

   ✓ Add or Subtract "like" terms using order of operation.

Example:

1) Simplify this expression. $4x(6x - 3) =$

   Use Distributive Property: $4x(6x - 3) = 24x^2 - 12x$

2) Simplify this expression. $(6x - 2)(2x - 3) =$

   First apply FOIL method: $(a + b)(c + d) = ac + ad + bc + bd$

   $(6x - 2)(2x - 3) = 12x^2 - 18x - 4x + 6$

   Now combine like terms: $12x^2 - 18x - 4x + 6 = 12x^2 - 22x + 6$

✍ ***Simplify each expression.***

1) $5(2x - 10) =$

2) $2x(4x - 2) =$

3) $4x(5x - 3) =$

4) $3x(7x + 3) =$

5) $4x(8x - 4) =$

6) $5x(5x + 4) =$

7) $(2x - 3)(x - 4) =$

8) $(x - 5)(3x + 4) =$

9) $(x - 5)(x - 3) =$

10) $(3x + 8)(3x - 8) =$

11) $(3x - 8)(3x - 4) =$

12) $3x^2 + 3x^2 - 2x^3 =$

Adding and Subtracting Polynomials

Step-by-step guide:

- ✓ Adding polynomials is just a matter of combining like terms, with some order of operations considerations thrown in.
- ✓ Be careful with the minus signs, and don't confuse addition and multiplication!

Example:

1) Simplify the expressions. $(4x^3 + 3x^4) - (x^4 - 5x^3) =$

   First use Distributive Property for $-(x^4 - 5x^3)$, $\rightarrow -(x^4 - 5x^3) = -x^4 + 5x^3$

   $(4x^3 + 3x^4) - (x^4 - 5x^3) = 4x^3 + 3x^4 - x^4 + 5x^3$

   Now combine like terms: $4x^3 + 3x^4 - x^4 + 5x^3 = 2x^4 + 9\quad^3$

2) Add expressions. $(2x^3 - 6) + (9x^3 - 4x^2) =$

   Remove parentheses: $(2x^3 - 6) + (9x^3 - 4x^2) = 2x^3 - 6 + 9x^3 - 4x^2$

   Now combine like terms: $2x^3 - 6 + 9x^3 - 4x^2 = 11x^3 - 4x^2 - 6$

✎ *Add or subtract expressions.*

1) $(-x^2 - 2) + (2x^2 + 1) =$

2) $(2x^2 + 3) - (3 - 4x^2) =$

3) $(2x^3 + 3x^2) - (x^3 + 8) =$

4) $(4x^3 - x^2) + (3x^2 - 5x) =$

5) $(7x^3 + 9x) - (3x^3 + 2) =$

6) $(2x^3 - 2) + (2x^3 + 2) =$

7) $(4x^3 + 5) - (7 - 2x^3) =$

8) $(4x^2 + 2x^3) - (2x^3 + 5) =$

9) $(4x^2 - x) + (3x - 5x^2) =$

10) $(7x + 9) - (3x + 9) =$

11) $(4x^4 - 2x) - (6x - 2x^4) =$

12) $(12x - 4x^3) - (8x^3 + 6x) =$

Answers – Day 20

Writing Polynomials in Standard Form

1) $2x$

2) -3

3) $-5x^3 + 3x^{-2}$

4) $4x^3$

5) $-6x^3 + 2x^2 + x$

6) $2x^3 - x^2$

7) $4x^3 - 2x^2 + 2x$

8) $-6x^3 - 2x^2 + 4x$

9) $2x^2 - 5x + 2$

10) $9x^4 - 7x + 12$

11) $-2x^3 + 5x^2 + 13x$

12) $-x^3 + 6x^2 + 10$

Simplifying Polynomials

1) $10x - 50$

2) $8x^2 - 4x$

3) $20x^2 - 12x$

4) $21x^2 + 9x$

5) $32x^2 - 16x$

6) $25x^2 + 20x$

7) $2x^2 - 11x + 12$

8) $3x^2 - 11x - 20$

9) $x^2 - 8x + 15$

10) $9x^2 - 64$

11) $9x^2 - 36x + 32$

12) $-2x^3 + 6x^2$

Adding and Subtracting Polynomials

1) $x^2 - 1$

2) $6x^2$

3) $x^3 + 3x^2 - 8$

4) $4x^3 + 2x^2 - 5x$

5) $4x^3 + 9x - 2$

6) $4x^3$

7) $6x^3 - 2$

8) $4x^2 - 5$

9) $-x^2 + 2x$

10) $4x$

11) $6x^4 - 8x$

12) $-12x^3 + 6x$

Day 21:
Monomials Operations

Math Topics that you'll learn today:

✓ Multiplying Monomials

✓ Multiplying and Dividing Monomials

✓ Multiplying a Polynomial and a Monomial

Mathematics is, I believe, the chief source of the belief in eternal and exact truth, as well as a sensible intelligible world. ~ Bertrand Russell

Multiplying Monomials

Step-by-step guide:

✓ A monomial is a polynomial with just one term, like $2x$ or $7y$.

Example:

1) Multiply expressions. $5a^4b^3 \times 2a^3b^2 =$

   Use this formula: $x^a \times x^b = x^{a+b}$

   $a^4 \times a^3 = a^{4+3} = a^7$ and $b^3 \times b^2 = b^{3+2} = b^5$

   Then: $5a^4b^3 \times 2a^3b^2 = 10a^7b^5$

2) Multiply expressions. $-4xy^4z^2 \times 3x^2y^5z^3 =$

   Use this formula: $x^a \times x^b = x^{a+b}$

   $x \times x^2 = x^{1+2} = x^3$, $y^4 \times y^5 = y^{4+5} = y^9$ and $z^2 \times z^3 = z^{2+3} = z^5$

   Then: $-4xy^4z^2 \times 3x^2y^5z^3 = -12x^3y^9z^5$

✍ *Simplify each expression.*

1) $4u^9 \times (-2u^3) =$

2) $(-2p^7) \times (-3p^2) =$

3) $3xy^2z^3 \times 2z^2 =$

4) $5u^5t \times 3ut^2 =$

5) $(-9a^6) \times (-5a^2b^4) =$

6) $-2a^3b^2 \times 4a^2b =$

7) $2xy^2 \times x^2y^3 =$

8) $3p^2q^4 \times (-2pq^3) =$

9) $4s^5t^2 \times 4st^3 =$

10) $(-6x^3y^2) \times 3x^2y =$

11) $2xy^2z \times 4z^2 =$

12) $4xy \times x^2y =$

Multiplying and Dividing Monomials

Step-by-step guide:

- ✓ When you divide two monomials you need to divide their coefficients and then divide their variables.
- ✓ In case of exponents with the same base, you need to subtract their powers.
- ✓ Exponent's rules:

$$x^a \times x^b = x^{a+b}, \qquad \frac{x^a}{x^b} = x^{a-b}$$
$$\frac{1}{x^b} = x^{-b}, \quad (x^a)^b = x^{a \times b}$$
$$(xy)^a = x^a \times y^a$$

Example:

1) Multiply expressions. $(-3x^7)(4x^3) =$
Use this formula: $x^a \times x^b = x^{a+b} \rightarrow x^7 \times x^3 = x^{10}$
Then: $(-3x^7)(4x^3) = -12x^{10}$

2) Dividing expressions. $\frac{18x^2y^5}{2xy^4} =$
Use this formula: $\frac{x^a}{x^b} = x^{a-b}$, $\frac{x^2}{x} = x^{2-1} = x$ and $\frac{y^5}{y^4} = y^{5-4} = y$
Then: $\frac{18x^2y^5}{2xy^4} = 9xy$

✎ *Simplify each expression.*

1) $(-2x^3y^4)(3x^3y^2) =$

2) $(-5x^3y^2)(-2x^4y^5) =$

3) $(9x^5y)(-3x^3y^3) =$

4) $(8x^7y^2)(6x^5y^4) =$

5) $(7x^4y^6)(4x^3y^4) =$

6) $(12x^2y^9)(7x^9y^{12}) =$

7) $\frac{12\ ^6y^8}{4x^4y^2} =$

8) $\frac{26x^9y^5}{2x^3y^4} =$

9) $\frac{80x^{12}y^9}{10x^6y^7} =$

10) $\frac{95x^{18}y^7}{5x^9y^2} =$

11) $\frac{200x^3y^8}{40x^3y^7} =$

12) $\frac{-15x^{17}y^{13}}{3x^6y^9} =$

Multiplying a Polynomial and a Monomial

Step-by-step guide:

✓ When multiplying monomials, use the product rule for exponents.

✓ When multiplying a monomial by a polynomial, use the distributive property.

$$a \times (b + c) = a \times b + a \times c$$

Example:

1) Multiply expressions. $-4x(5x + 9) =$

Use Distributive Property: $-4x(5x + 9) = -20x^2 - 36x$

2) Multiply expressions. $2x(6x^2 - 3y^2) =$

Use Distributive Property: $2x(6x^2 - 3y^2) = 12x^3 - 6xy^2$

✎ *Find each product.*

1) $3x(9x + 2y) =$

2) $6x(x + 2y) =$

3) $9x(2x + 4y) =$

4) $12x(3x + 9) =$

5) $11x(2x - 11y) =$

6) $2x(6x - 6y) =$

7) $2x(3x - 6y + 3) =$

8) $5x(3x^2 + 2y^2) =$

9) $13x(4x + 8y) =$

10) $5(2x^2 - 9y^2) =$

11) $3x(-2x^2y + 3y) =$

12) $-2(2x^2 - 2xy + 2) =$

Answers – Day 21

Multiplying Monomials

1) $-8u^{12}$
2) $6p^9$
3) $6xy^2z^5$
4) $15u^6t^3$
5) $45a^8b^4$
6) $-8a^5b^3$
7) $2x^3y^5$
8) $-6p^3q^7$
9) $16s^6t^5$
10) $-18x^5y^3$
11) $8xy^2z^3$
12) $4x^3y^2$

Multiplying and Dividing Monomials

1) $-6x^6y^6$
2) $10x^7y^7$
3) $-27x^8y^4$
4) $48x^{12}y^6$
5) $28x^7y^{10}$
6) $84x^{11}y^{21}$
7) $3x^2y^6$
8) $13x^6y$
9) $8x^6y^2$
10) $19x^9y^5$
11) $5y$
12) $-5x^{11}y^4$

Multiplying a Polynomial and a Monomial

1) $27x^2 + 6xy$
2) $6x^2 + 12xy$
3) $18x^2 + 36xy$
4) $36x^2 + 108x$
5) $22x^2 - 121xy$
6) $12x^2 - 12xy$
7) $6x^2 - 12xy + 6x$
8) $15x^3 + 10xy^2$
9) $52x^2 + 104xy$
10) $10x^2 - 45y^2$
11) $-6x^3y + 9xy$
12) $-4x^2 + 4xy - 4$

Day 22:
Polynomials Operations

Math Topics that you'll learn today:

- ✓ Multiplying Binomials

- ✓ Factoring Trinomials

- ✓ Operations with Polynomials

Mathematics compares the most diverse phenomena and discovers the secret analogies that unite them. ~ Joseph Fourier

Multiplying Binomials

Step-by-step guide:

✓ Use "FOIL". (First-Out-In-Last)
$$(x + a)(x + b) = x^2 + (b + a)x + ab$$

Example:

1) Multiply Binomials. $(x - 2)(x + 2) =$

Use "FOIL". (First–Out–In–Last): $(x - 2)(x + 2) = x^2 + 2x - 2x - 4$

Then simplify: $x^2 + 2x - 2x - 4 = {}^2 - 4$

2) Multiply Binomials. $(x + 5)(x - 2) =$

Use "FOIL". (First–Out–In–Last):

$(x + 5)(x - 2) = x^2 - 2x + 5x - 10$

Then simplify: $x^2 - 2x + 5x - 10 = x^2 + 3x - 10$

✍ *Find each product.*

1) $(x + 2)(x + 2) =$

2) $(x - 3)(x + 2) =$

3) $(x - 2)(x - 4) =$

4) $(x + 3)(x + 2) =$

5) $(x - 4)(x - 5) =$

6) $(x + 5)(x + 2) =$

7) $(x - 6)(x + 3) =$

8) $(x - 8)(x - 4) =$

9) $(x + 2)(x + 8) =$

10) $(x - 2)(x + 4) =$

11) $(x + 4)(x + 4) =$

12) $(x + 5)(x + 5) =$

Factoring Trinomials

Step-by-step guide:

✓ "FOIL":
$$(x + a)(x + b) = x^2 + (b + a)x + ab$$

✓ "Difference of Squares":
$$a^2 - b^2 = (a + b)(a - b)$$
$$a^2 + 2ab + b^2 = (a + b)(a + b)$$
$$a^2 - 2ab + b^2 = (a - b)(a - b)$$

✓ "Reverse FOIL":
$$x^2 + (b + a)x + ab = (x + a)(x + b)$$

Example:

1) Factor this trinomial. $x^2 - 2x - 8 =$
   Break the expression into groups: $(x^2 + 2x) + (-4x - 8)$
   Now factor out x from $x^2 + 2x$: $x(x + 2)$ and factor out -4 from $-4x - 8$: $-4(x + 2)$
   Then: $= x(x + 2) - 4(x + 2)$, now factor out like term: $x + 2$
   Then: $(x + 2)(x - 4)$

2) Factor this trinomial. $x^2 - 6x + 8 =$
   Break the expression into groups: $(x^2 - 2x) + (-4x + 8)$
   Now factor out x from $x^2 - 2x$: $x(x - 2)$, and factor out -4 from $-4x + 8$: $-4(x - 2)$
   Then: $= x(x - 2) - 4(x - 2)$, now factor out like term: $x - 2$
   Then: $(x - 2)(x - 4)$

✎ *Factor each trinomial.*

1) $x^2 + 8x + 15 =$

2) $x^2 - 5x + 6 =$

3) $x^2 + 6x + 8 =$

4) $x^2 - 8x + 16 =$

5) $x^2 - 7x + 12 =$

6) $x^2 + 11x + 18 =$

7) $x^2 + 2x - 24 =$

8) $x^2 + 4x - 12 =$

9) $x^2 - 10x + 9 =$

10) $x^2 + 5x - 14 =$

11) $x^2 - 6x - 27 =$

12) $x^2 - 11x - 42 =$

Operations with Polynomials

Step-by-step guide:

✓ When multiplying a monomial by a polynomial, use the distributive property.

$$a \times (b + c) = a \times b + a \times$$

Example:

1) Multiply. $5(2x - 6) =$

Use the distributive property: $5(2x - 6) = 10x - 30$

2) Multiply. $2x(6x + 2) =$

Use the distributive property: $2x(6 + 2) = 12x^2 + 4x$

✎ *Find each product.*

1) $9(6x + 2) =$

2) $8(3x + 7) =$

3) $5(6x - 1) =$

4) $-3(8x - 3) =$

5) $3x^2(6x - 5) =$

6) $5x^2(7x - 2) =$

7) $6x^3(-3x + 4) =$

8) $-7x^4(2x - 4) =$

9) $8(x^2 + 2x - 3) =$

10) $4(4x^2 - 2x + 1) =$

11) $2(3x^2 + 2x - 2) =$

12) $8x(5x^2 + 3x + 8) =$

Answers – Day 22

Multiplying Binomials

1) $x^2 + 4x + 4$

2) $x^2 - x - 6$

3) $x^2 - 6x + 8$

4) $x^2 + 5x + 6$

5) $x^2 - 9x + 20$

6) $x^2 + 7x + 10$

7) $x^2 - 3x - 18$

8) $x^2 - 12x + 32$

9) $x^2 + 10x + 16$

10) $x^2 + 2x - 8$

11) $x^2 + 8x + 16$

12) $x^2 + 10x + 25$

Factoring Trinomials

1) $(x + 3)(x + 5)$

2) $(x - 2)(x - 3)$

3) $(x + 4)(x + 2)$

4) $(x - 4)(x - 4)$

5) $(x - 3)(x - 4)$

6) $(x + 2)(x + 9)$

7) $(x + 6)(x - 4)$

8) $(x - 2)(x + 6)$

9) $(x - 1)(x - 9)$

10) $(x - 2)(x + 7)$

11) $(x - 9)(x + 3)$

12) $(x + 3)(x - 14)$

Operations with Polynomials

1) $54x + 18$

2) $24x + 56$

3) $30x - 5$

4) $-24x + 9$

5) $18x^3 - 15x^2$

6) $35x^3 - 10x^2$

7) $-18x^4 + 24x^3$

8) $-14x^5 + 28x^4$

9) $8x^2 + 16x - 24$

10) $16x^2 - 8x + 4$

11) $6x^2 + 4x - 4$

12) $40x^3 + 24x^2 + 64x$

Day 23:
System of Equations

Math Topics that you'll learn today:

- ✓ Solving Systems of Equations
- ✓ Systems of Equations Word Problems

Mathematics is a hard thing to love. It has the unfortunate habit, like a rude dog, of turning its most unfavorable side towards you when you first make contact with it. ~ David Whiteland

Systems of Equations

Step-by-step guide:

- ✓ A system of equations contains two equations and two variables. For example, consider the system of equations: $x - y = 1, x + y = 5$
- ✓ The easiest way to solve a system of equation is using the elimination method. The elimination method uses the addition property of equality. You can add the same value to each side of an equation.
- ✓ For the first equation above, you can add $x + y$ to the left side and 5 to the right side of the first equation: $x - y + (x + y) = 1 + 5$. Now, if you simplify, you get: $x - y + (x + y) = 1 + 5 \rightarrow 2x = 6 \rightarrow x = 3$. Now, substitute 3 for the x in the first equation: $3 - y = 1$. By solving this equation, $y = 2$

Example:

What is the value of $x + y$ in this system of equations? $\begin{cases} 3x - 4y = -20 \\ -x + 2y = 10 \end{cases}$

Solving Systems of Equations by Elimination: $\begin{array}{r} 3x - 4y = -20 \\ -x + 2y = 10 \\ \hline \end{array}$ ⇒ Multiply the second equation by 3, then add it to the first equation.

$\begin{array}{r} 3x - 4y = -20 \\ 3(-x + 2y = 10) \\ \hline \end{array} \Rightarrow \begin{array}{r} 3x - 4y = -20 \\ -3x + 6y = 30) \\ \hline \end{array} \Rightarrow 2y = 10 \Rightarrow y = 5.$ Now, substitute 5 for y in the first equation and solve for x. $3x - 4(5) = -20 \rightarrow 3x - 20 = -20 \rightarrow x = 0$

✍ *Solve each system of equations.*

1) $-2x + 2y = 4$ $x =$ ____

   $-2x + y = 3$ $y =$ ____

2) $-10x + 2y = -6$ $x =$ ____

   $6x - 16y = 48$ $y =$ ____

3) $y = -8$ $x =$ ____

   $16x - 12y = 32$

4) $2y = -6x + 10$ $x =$ ____

   $10x - 8y = -6$ $y =$ ____

5) $10x - 9y = -13$ $x =$ ____

   $-5x + 3y = 11$ $y =$ ____

6) $-3x - 4y = 5$ $x =$ ____

   $x - 2y = 5$ $y =$ ____

Systems of Equations Word Problems

Step-by-step guide:

✓ Define your variables, write two equations, and use elimination method for solving systems of equations.

Example:

Tickets to a movie cost $8 for adults and $5 for students. A group of friends purchased **20** tickets for $**115.00**. How many adults ticket did they buy? _____

Let x be the number of adult tickets and y be the number of student tickets. There are 20 tickets. Then: $x + y = 20$. The cost of adults' tickets is $8 and for students it is $5, and the total cost is $115. So, $8x + 5y = 20$. Now, we have a system of equations: $\begin{cases} x + y = 20 \\ 8x + 5y = 115 \end{cases}$

Multiply the first equation by -5 and add to the second equation: $-5(x + y = 20) = -5x - 5y = -100$

$8x + 5y + (-5x - 5y) = 115 - 100 \rightarrow 3x = 15 \rightarrow x = 5 \rightarrow 5 + y = 20 \rightarrow y = 15$. There are 5 adult tickets and 15 student tickets.

✎ *Solve each word problem.*

1) Tickets to a movie cost $5 for adults and $3 for students. A group of friends purchased **18** tickets for $**82.00**. How many adults ticket did they buy? _____

2) At a store, Eva bought two shirts and five hats for $**154.00**. Nicole bought three same shirts and four same hats for $**168.00**. What is the price of each shirt? _____

3) A farmhouse shelters **10** animals, some are pigs, and some are ducks. Altogether there are 36 legs. How many pigs are there? _____

4) A class of **195** students went on a field trip. They took **19** vehicles, some cars and some buses. If each car holds 5 students and each bus hold 25 students, how many buses did they take? _____

Answers – Day 23

Systems of Equations

1) $x = -1, y = 1$
2) $x = 0, y = -3$
3) $x = -4$
4) $x = 1, y = 2$
5) $x = -4, y = -3$
6) $x = 1, y = -2$

Systems of Equations Word Problems

1) 14
2) $32
3) 8
4) 5

Day 24:
Triangles and Polygons

Math Topics that you'll learn today:

- ✓ The Pythagorean Theorem

- ✓ Triangles

- ✓ Polygons

Mathematics is like checkers in being suitable for the young, not too difficult, amusing, and without peril to the state. ~ Plato

The Pythagorean Theorem

Step-by-step guide:

✓ In any right triangle: $a^2 + b^2 = c^2$

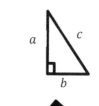

Example:

1) Find the missing length.

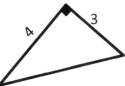

Use Pythagorean Theorem: $a^2 + b^2 = c^2$

Then: $a^2 + b^2 = c^2 \rightarrow 3^2 + 4^2 = c^2 \rightarrow 9 + 16 = c^2$

$c^2 = 25 \rightarrow c = 5$

2) Right triangle ABC has two legs of lengths 6 cm (AB) and 8 cm (AC). What is the length of the third side (BC)?

Use Pythagorean Theorem: $a^2 + b^2 = c^2$

Then: $a^2 + b^2 = c^2 \rightarrow 6^2 + 8^2 = c^2 \rightarrow 36 + 64 = c^2$

$c^2 = 100 \rightarrow c = 10$

✎ *Find the missing side?*

1)	2)	3)	4)
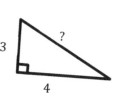		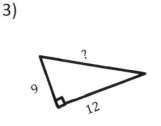	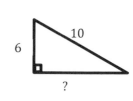

5)	6)	7)	8)
	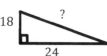	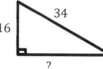	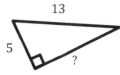

Triangles

Step-by-step guide:

✓ In any triangle the sum of all angles is 180 degrees.
✓ Area of a triangle = $\frac{1}{2} (base \times height)$

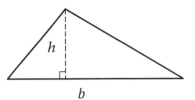

Example:

What is the area of triangles?

1)

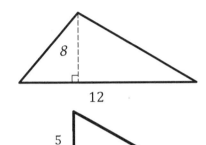

2)

Solution:

Use the are formula: Area $= \frac{1}{2} (base \times height)$
$base = 12$ and $height = 8$
Area $= \frac{1}{2}(12 \times 8) = \frac{1}{2}(96) = 48$

Solution:

Use the are formula: Area $= \frac{1}{2} (base \times height)$
$base = 6$ and $height = 5$
Area $= \frac{1}{2}(5 \times 6) = \frac{30}{2} = 15$

✍ *Find the measure of the unknown angle in each triangle.*

1)

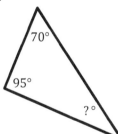

2)

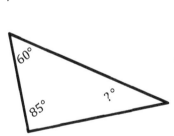

3)

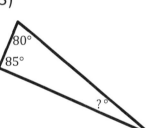

4)

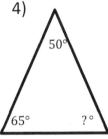

✍ *Find area of each triangle.*

5)

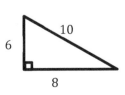

6)

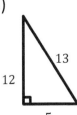

7)

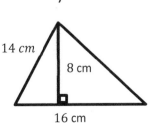

8)

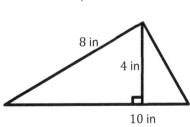

Polygons

Step-by-step guide:

Perimeter of a square $= 4 \times side = 4s$

 s

Perimeter of a rectangle

$= 2(width + length)$ width

length

Perimeter of trapezoid

$= a + b + c + d$

Perimeter of a regular hexagon $= 6a$

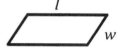 a

---

Example: Find the perimeter of following regular hexagon.

3 m

3 m   3 m

Perimeter of Pentagon $= 6a$

Perimeter of Pentagon $= 6a = 6 \times 3 = 18m$

Perimeter of a parallelogram $= 2(l + w)$

l

w

✎ *Find the perimeter of each shape.*

1)

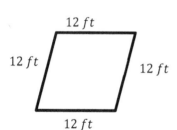

12 ft
12 ft   12 ft
12 ft

2)

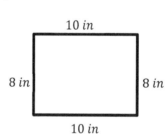

10 in
8 in   8 in
10 in

3)

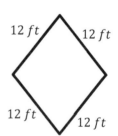

12 ft   12 ft

12 ft   12 ft

4)

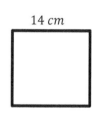

14 cm

---

5) Regular hexagon

5 m

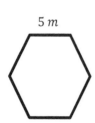

6)

4.5 cm
5.5 cm
4 cm
5.5 cm
4.5 cm

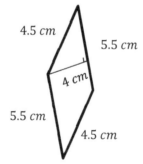

7) Parallelogram

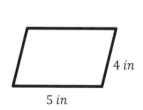

4 in

5 in

8) Square

6 m

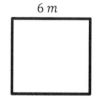

132

Answers – Day 24

The Pythagorean Theorem

1) 5

2) 17

3) 15

4) 8

5) 5

6) 30

7) 30

8) 12

Triangles

1) 15°
2) 35°
3) 15°
4) 65°
5) 24 *square unites*

6) 30 *square unites*

7) 64 *square unites*

8) 20 *square unites*

Polygons

1) 48 *ft*

2) 36 *in*

3) 48 *ft*

4) 56 *cm*

5) 30 *m*

6) 20 *cm*

7) 18 *in*

8) 24 *m*

Day 25:
Circles, Trapezoids and Cubes

Math Topics that you'll learn today:

✓ Circles

✓ Trapezoids

✓ Cubes

Mathematics is as much an aspect of culture as it is a collection of algorithms. ~ Carl Boyer

Circles

Step-by-step guide:

- ✓ In a circle, variable r is usually used for the radius and d for diameter and π is about 3.14.
- ✓ *Area of a circle* $= \pi r^2$
- ✓ *Circumference of a circle* $= 2\pi r$

Example:

1) Find the area of the circle.

Use area formula: $Area = \pi r^2$,

$r = 4$ then: $Area = \pi(4)^2 = 14\pi$, $\pi = 3.14$ then: $Area = 14 \times 3.14 = 43.96$

2) Find the Circumference of the circle.

Use Circumference formula: $Circumference = 2\pi r$

$r = 6$, then: $Circumference = 2\pi(6) = 12\pi$

$\pi = 3.14$ then: $Circumference = 12 \times 3.14 = 37.68$

✍ ***Complete the table below.*** ($\pi = 3.14$)

	Radius	Diameter	Circumference	Area
Circle 1	4 inches	8 inches	25.12 inches	50.24 square inches
Circle 2		12 meters		
Circle 3				12.56 square ft
Circle 4			18.84 miles	
Circle 5		5 kilometers		
Circle 6	6 centimeters			
Circle 7		8 feet		
Circle 8				28.26 square meters

Trapezoids

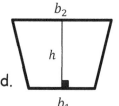

Step-by-step guide:

   ✓ A quadrilateral with at least one pair of parallel sides is a trapezoid.
   ✓ Area of a trapezoid $= \frac{1}{2}h(b_1 + b_2)$

Example:

Calculate the area of the trapezoid.

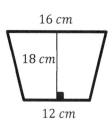

Use area formula: $A = \frac{1}{2}h(b_1 + b_2)$

$b_1 = 12$, $b_2 = 16$ and $h = 18$

Then: $A = \frac{1}{2}18(12 + 16) = 9(28) = 252\ cm^2$

✎ *Find the area of each trapezoid.*

1)
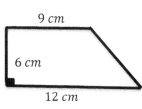

2)
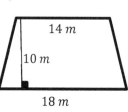

3)
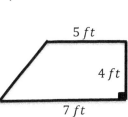

4)
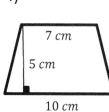

5)
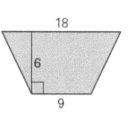

6)
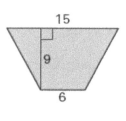

7)
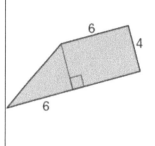

8)
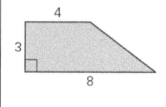

Cubes

Step-by-step guide:

- ✓ A cube is a three-dimensional solid object bounded by six square sides.
- ✓ Volume is the measure of the amount of space inside of a solid figure, like a cube, ball, cylinder or pyramid.
- ✓ Volume of a cube = $(one\ side)^3$
- ✓ surface area of cube = $6 \times (one\ side)^2$

Example:

Find the volume and surface area of this cube.

2 cm

Use volume formula: $volume = (one\ side)^3$

Then: $volume = (one\ side)^3 = (2)^3 = 8\ cm^3$

Use surface area formula:

$surface\ area\ of\ cube$: $6(one\ side)^2 = 6(2)^2 = 6(4) = 24\ cm^2$

✍ *Find the volume of each cube.*

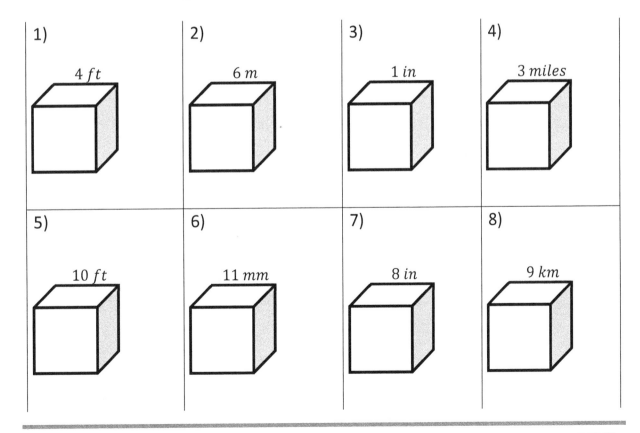

1) 4 ft

2) 6 m

3) 1 in

4) 3 miles

5) 10 ft

6) 11 mm

7) 8 in

8) 9 km

Answers – Day 25

Circles

	Radius	Diameter	Circumference	Area
Circle 1	4 *inches*	8 *inches*	25.12 *inches*	50.24 *square inches*
Circle 2	6 *meters*	12 *meters*	37.68 *meters*	113.04 *meters*
Circle 3	2 *square ft*	4 *square ft*	12.56 *square ft*	12.56 *square ft*
Circle 4	3 *miles*	6 *miles*	18.84 *miles*	28.26 *miles*
Circle 5	2.5 *kilometers*	5 *kilometers*	15.7 *kilometers*	19.63 *kilometers*
Circle 6	6 *centimeters*	12 *centimeters*	37.68 *centimeters*	113.04 *centimeters*
Circle 7	4 *feet*	8 *feet*	25.12 *feet*	50.24 *feet*
Circle 8	3 *square meters*	6 *square meters*	18.84 *square meters*	28.26 *square meters*

Trapezoids

1) $63\ cm^2$
2) $160\ m^2$
3) $24\ ft^2$
4) $42.5\ cm^2$
5) 81
6) 94.5
7) 36
8) 18

Cubes

1) $64\ ft^3$
2) $216\ m^3$
3) $1\ in^3$
4) $27\ miles^3$
5) $1,000\ ft^3$
6) $1,331\ mm^3$
7) $512\ in^3$
8) $729\ km^3$

Day 26:
Rectangular Prisms and Cylinder

Math Topics that you'll learn today:

✓ Rectangle Prisms

✓ Cylinder

It's fine to work on any problem, so long as it generates interesting mathematics along the way - even if you don't solve it at the end of the day." ~ Andrew Wiles

Rectangular Prisms

Step-by-step guide:

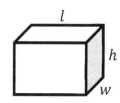

✓ A solid 3-dimensional object which has six rectangular faces.
✓ Volume of a Rectangular prism = **Length × Width × Height**

$Volume = l \times w \times h$ $Surface\ area = 2(wh + lw + lh)$

Example:

Find the volume and surface area of rectangular prism.

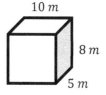

Use volume formula: $Volume = l \times w \times h$

Then: $Volume = 10 \times 5 \times 8 = 400\ m^3$

Use surface area formula: $Surface\ area = 2(wh + lw + lh)$

Then: $Surface\ area = 2(5 \times 8 + 10 \times 5 + 10 \times 8) = 2(40 + 50 + 80) = 340\ m^2$

 Find the volume of each Rectangular Prism.

1)

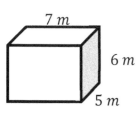

2)

7 m
6 m
5 m

10 in
8 in
4 in

3)

9 m
7 m
3 m

4)

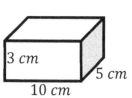

3 cm
5 cm
10 cm

5)

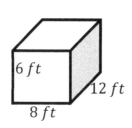

6 ft
12 ft
8 ft

6)

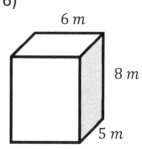

6 m
8 m
5 m

Cylinder

Step-by-step guide:

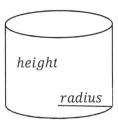

- ✓ A cylinder is a solid geometric figure with straight parallel sides and a circular or oval cross section.
- ✓ *Volume of Cylinder Formula* $= \pi(radius)^2 \times height \ \pi = 3.14$
- ✓ *Surface area of a cylinder* $= 2\pi r^2 + 2\pi rh$

Example:

Find the volume and Surface area of the follow Cylinder.

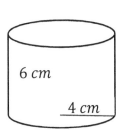

Use volume formula: $Volume = \pi(radius)^2 \times height$

Then: $Volume = \pi(4)^2 \times 6 = \pi 16 \times 6 = 96\pi$

$\pi = 3.14$ then: $Volume = 96\pi = 301.44$

Use surface area formula: $Surface\ area = 2\pi r^2 + 2\pi rh$

Then: $= 2\pi(4)^2 + 2\pi(4)(6) = 2\pi(16) + 2\pi(24) = 32\pi + 48\pi = 80\pi$

$\pi = 3.14$ then: $Surface\ area = 80 \times 3.14 = 251.2$

✎ **Find the volume of each Cylinder. Round your answer to the nearest tenth.** ($\pi = 3.14$)

1)

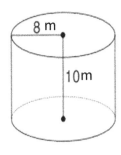

8 m

10m

2)

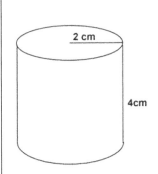

2 cm

4cm

3)

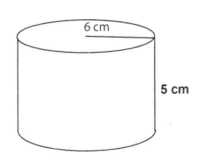

6 cm

5 cm

4)

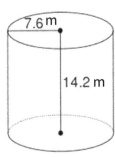

7.6 m

14.2 m

5)

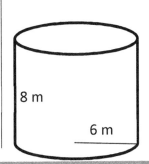

8 m

6 m

6)

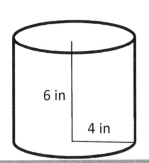

6 in

4 in

Answers – Day 26

Rectangle Prisms

1) $210 \ m^3$
2) $320 \ in^3$
3) $189 \ m^3$

4) $150 \ cm^3$
5) $576 \ ft^3$
6) $240 \ m^3$

Cylinder

1) $2,009.6 \ m^3$
2) $50.24 \ cm^3$
3) $565.2 \ cm^3$

4) $2,575.4 \ m^3$
5) $904.3 \ m^3$
6) $301.4 \ in^3$

Day 27: Statistics

Math Topics that you'll learn today:

✓ Mean, Median, Mode, and Range of the Given Data

✓ Histograms

Millions saw the apple fall, but Newton asked why." – Bernard Baruch

Mean, Median, Mode, and Range of the Given Data

Step-by-step guide:

- ✓ Mean: $\dfrac{\text{sum of the data}}{\text{total number of data entires}}$
- ✓ Mode: value in the list that appears most often
- ✓ Range: the difference of largest value and smallest value in the list

Example:

1) What is the median of these numbers? $4, 9, 13, 8, 15, 18, 5$

   Write the numbers in order: $4, 5, 8, 9, 13, 15, 18$

   Median is the number in the middle. Therefore, the median is 9.

2) What is the mode of these numbers? $22, 16, 12, 9, 7, 6, 4, 6$

   Mode: value in the list that appears most often
   Therefore: mode is 6

✍ *Solve.*

1) In a javelin throw competition, five athletics score $56, 58, 63, 57$ and 61 meters. What are their Mean and Median? _____

2) Eva went to shop and bought 3 apples, 5 peaches, 8 bananas, 1 pineapple and 3 melons. What are the Mean and Median of her purchase? _____

✍ *Find Mode and Rage of the Given Data.*

3) $8, 2, 5, 9, 1, 2$

   Mode: _____   Range: _____

4) $4, 4, 3, 9, 7, 9, 4, 6, 4$

   Mode: _____   Range: _____

5) $6, 6, 2, 3, 6, 3, 9, 12$

   Mode: _____   Range: _____

6) $12, 9, 2, 9, 3, 2, 9, 5$

   Mode: _____   Range: _____

Histograms

Step-by-step guide:

✓ A histogram is an accurate representation of the distribution of numerical data.

Example:

Use the following Graph to complete the table.

Answer:

Day	Distance (km)
1	
2	

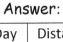

Day	Distance (km)
1	359
2	460
3	278
4	547
5	360

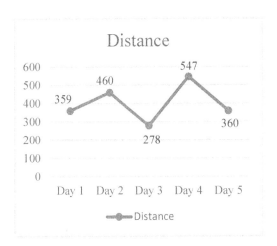

✎ The following table shows the number of births in the US from 2007 to 2012 (in millions).

Year	Number of births (in millions)
2007	4.32
2008	4.25
2009	4.13
2010	4
2011	3.95
2012	3.95

Draw a histogram for the table.

Answers – Day 27

Mean, Median, Mode, and Range of the Given Data

1) Mean: 59, Median: 58

2) Mean: 4, Median: 3

3) Mode: 2, Range: 8

4) Mode: 6, Range: 10

5) Mode: 4, Range: 6

6) Mode: 9, Range: 10

Histograms

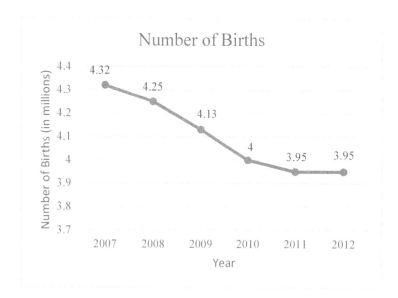

Day 28: Data and Probability

Math Topics that you'll learn today:

✓ Pie Graph

✓ Probability

Mathematics is the supreme judge; from its decisions there is no appeal.

~Tobias Dantzig

Pie Graph

Step-by-step guide:

✓ A Pie Chart is a circle chart divided into sectors, each sector represents the relative size of each value.

Example:

A library has 840 books that include Mathematics, Physics, Chemistry, English and History. Use following graph to answer question.

What is the number of Mathematics books?

Number of total books = 840,
Percent of Mathematics books = 30% = 0.30
Then: $0.30 \times 840 = 252$

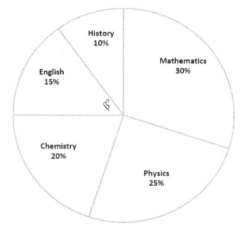

✍ **The circle graph below shows all Jason's expenses for last month. Jason spent $300 on his bills last month.**

1) How much did Jason spend on his car last month? _____

2) How much did Jason spend for foods last month? _____

3) How much did Jason spend on his rent last month? _____

4) What fraction is Jason's expenses for his bills and Car out of his total expenses last month?

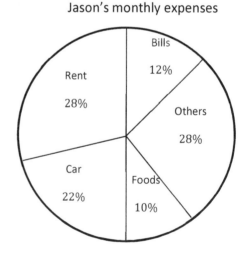

Jason's monthly expenses

Probability Problems

Step-by-step guide:

- ✓ Probability is the likelihood of something happening in the future. It is expressed as a number between zero (can never happen) to 1 (will always happen).
- ✓ Probability can be expressed as a fraction, a decimal, or a percent.

Example:

1) If there are 8 red balls and 12 blue balls in a basket, what is the probability that John will pick out a red ball from the basket?
   There are 8 red ball and 20 are total number of balls. Therefore, probability that John will pick out a red ball from the basket is 8 out of 20 or $\frac{8}{8+12} = \frac{8}{20} = \frac{2}{5}$.

2) A bag contains 18 balls: two green, five black, eight blue, a brown, a red and one white. If 17 balls are removed from the bag at random, what is the probability that a brown ball has been removed?
   If 17 balls are removed from the bag at random, there will be one ball in the bag.
   The probability of choosing a brown ball is 1 out of 18. Therefore, the probability of not choosing a brown ball is 17 out of 18 and the probability of having not a brown ball after removing 17 balls is the same.

✍ Solve.

1) A number is chosen at random from 1 to 10. Find the probability of selecting number 4 or smaller numbers. _____

2) Bag A contains 9 red marbles and 3 green marbles. Bag B contains 9 black marbles and 6 orange marbles. What is the probability of selecting a green marble at random from bag A? What is the probability of selecting a black marble at random from Bag B? _____ _____

Answers – Day 28

Pie Graph

1) $550
2) $250
3) $700
4) $\frac{17}{50}$

Probability Problems

1) $\frac{2}{5}$
2) $\frac{1}{4}, \frac{3}{5}$

Day 29: Time to Test

TABE Test Review

The Test of Adult Basic Education, or TABE, is a diagnostic test to determine a person's skill levels and aptitudes. It measures reading, math, and English skills required by many local employers or for application to certain programs.

There are several versions of the TABE test. The complete battery TABE test consists of 195 multiple-choice questions, while the smaller survey TABE only contains 100 questions.

The TABE test consists of four sections:

- o Reading
- o Language
- o Math Computation
- o Applied Math

The Computation section of the TABE Math measures your knowledge of Math operations (addition, subtraction, multiplication, and division) with numbers. There are 40 questions in this section, and you cannot use a calculator. The Applied Math section is an assessment of your knowledge of Math and consists of 50 questions. This section of the test covers basic mathematics topics, quantitative problem-solving and algebraic questions. You are allowed to use a calculator.

In days 29 and 30, there are two complete TABE Mathematics Tests. Take these tests to see what score you'll be able to receive on a real TABE test.

Good luck!

Time to refine your skill with a practice examination

Take a REAL TABE Mathematics test to simulate the test day experience. After you've finished, score your test using the answer key.

Before You Start

- You'll need a pencil, calculator, and a timer to take the test.

- It's okay to guess. You won't lose any points if you're wrong.

- After you've finished the test, review the answer key to see where you went wrong.

Calculators are permitted only for the second part of the test (Applied Math)

Good Luck!

Complete TABE Battery Math

Practice Test

2019

Two Parts

Total number of questions: 90

Part 1 (Non-Calculator) Math Computation: 40 questions

Part 2 (May use Calculator) Applied Math: 50 questions

Total time for two parts: 79 Minutes

Complete TABE Battery Math Practice Test

Part 1

Mathematics Computation

(Non-Calculator)

40 questions

Total time: 24 Minutes

1)
$$\begin{array}{r} 2{,}619 \\ -\ \ 511 \\ \hline \end{array}$$

☐A. 2,141   ☐B. 2,108

☐C. 2,907   ☐D. 2,198

2)
$$\begin{array}{r} 168 \\ +\ 6{,}678 \\ \hline \end{array}$$

☐A. 6,224   ☐B. 6,654

☐C. 6,465   ☐D. 6,846

3)
$$\begin{array}{r} 760 \\ +\ \ 13 \\ \hline \end{array}$$

☐A. 578   ☐B. 876

☐C. 773   ☐D. 786

4)
$$\begin{array}{r} 430 \\ -\ 141 \\ \hline \end{array}$$

☐A. 289   ☐B. 387

☐C. 141   ☐D. 257

5) $12 \times 6 =$

☐A. 40   ☐B. 60

☐C. 72   ☐D. 80

6) $\$1{,}383 + \$578 =$

☐A. $1,970   ☐B. $1,781

☐C. $1,166   ☐D. $1,188

7) $8{,}000 \div 250 =$

☐A. 22   ☐B. 32

☐C. 42   ☐D. 52

8) $3,521 − $1,563 =

☐A. $1,938   ☐B. $1,948

☐C. $1,942   ☐D. $1,958

9) $\begin{array}{r} 83.65 \\ +\ 13.38 \\ \hline \end{array}$

☐A. 84.95   ☐B. 94.84

☐C. 89.86   ☐D. 97.03

10) ___ + 4.2 = 9.6

☐A. 3.4   ☐B. 1.4

☐C. 2.4   ☐D. 5.4

11) 47.12 − 24.34 =

☐A. 12.78   ☐B. 15.68

☐C. 20.78   ☐D. 22.78

12) $\begin{array}{r} 6.2 \\ \times\ 3.3 \\ \hline \end{array}$

☐A. 8.11   ☐B. 14.46

☐C. 11.46   ☐D. 20.46

13) 15.6 ÷ 100 =

☐A. 0.156   ☐B. 0.0156

☐C. 0.00156   ☐D. 0.000156

14) 550 ÷ 5 =

☐A. 115   ☐B. 112

☐C. 110   ☐D. 105

15) $\frac{3}{7} + \frac{2}{7} =$

☐A. $\frac{1}{7}$ ☐B. $\frac{4}{14}$

☐C. $\frac{5}{7}$ ☐D. $\frac{2}{49}$

16) $12.6 \div 4.6 =$

☐A. 2.7   ☐B. 2.4

☐C. 2.6   ☐D. 2

17) $4\overline{)148}$

☐A. 33   ☐B. 35

☐C. 36   ☐D. 37

18) $8\overline{)2768}$

☐A. 241   ☐B. 346

☐C. 356   ☐D. 414

19) $\frac{4}{3} - \frac{2}{3} =$

☐A. $\frac{2}{3}$ ☐B. 2

☐C. $\frac{1}{3}$ ☐D. 1

20) $\frac{4}{5} + \frac{1}{5} =$

☐A. $\frac{4}{5}$ ☐B. 0

☐C. $\frac{1}{5}$ ☐D. 1

21) $5\frac{3}{2} + 8\frac{1}{3} =$

☐A. $3\frac{5}{6}$ ☐B. $14\frac{6}{5}$

☐C. $14\frac{5}{6}$ ☐D. $3\frac{6}{5}$

22) $6\frac{3}{5} - 2\frac{1}{5} =$

☐A. $4\frac{2}{5}$ ☐B. $3\frac{2}{5}$

☐C. $7\frac{1}{5}$ ☐D. $12\frac{1}{5}$

23) $5\frac{1}{3} - \frac{3}{4} =$

☐A. $5\frac{1}{12}$ ☐B. $4\frac{1}{12}$

☐C. $4\frac{11}{12}$ ☐D. $4\frac{7}{12}$

24) $\frac{2}{3} \times \frac{5}{7} =$

☐A. $\frac{2}{5}$ ☐B. $\frac{4}{15}$

☐C. $\frac{10}{21}$ ☐D. $\frac{4}{21}$

25) $\frac{3}{5} \div \frac{1}{10} =$

☐A. $\frac{4}{50}$ ☐B. $\frac{5}{50}$

☐C. $\frac{1}{50}$ ☐D. 6

26) $2\frac{4}{3} \times 2\frac{1}{6} =$

☐A. $7\frac{2}{9}$ ☐B. $5\frac{9}{7}$

☐C. $5\frac{7}{9}$ ☐D. $2\frac{9}{7}$

27) $12ab - 7ab =$

☐A. $19ab$ ☐B. $5ab$

☐C. $6ab$ ☐D. $15ab$

28) $4^2 \times 4^5 =$

☐A. 4^{10} ☐B. 4^7

☐C. 4^2 ☐D. 4^5

29) $4\frac{2}{5} \div 2\frac{6}{10} =$

☐A. $1\frac{9}{13}$ ☐B. $1\frac{13}{10}$

☐C. $\frac{10}{13}$ ☐D. $2\frac{13}{10}$

30) 4% of 20 =

☐A. 5   ☐B. 4

☐C. 2   ☐D. 0.8

31) 60% of 30 =

☐A. 24   ☐B. 20

☐C. 18   ☐D. 10

32) $17 - (-14) =$

☐A. 6   ☐B. 9

☐C. 31   ☐D. 20

33) ___% of 40 = 14

☐A. 15%   ☐B. 25%

☐C. 35%   ☐D. 50%

34) 8% of ___ = 72

☐A. 1,300   ☐B. 1,000

☐C. 900   ☐D. 800

35) $5x + 3x =$

☐A. $3x$ ☐B. $5x$

☐C. $8x$ ☐D. $10x$

36) $10 \times (-3) =$

☐A. -5 ☐B. -30

☐C. -10 ☐D. 30

37) $8ab - 3ab =$

☐A. ab ☐B. $5ab$

☐C. $11ab$ ☐D. $30ab$

38) $-3 + 5 + 3 =$

☐A. 5   ☐B. −5

☐C. 11   ☐D. −3

39) $9^7 \times 9^7 =$

☐A. 9^{49} ☐B. 81^{14}

☐C. 9^1 ☐D. 9^{14}

40) $160.35 \div 2.50 =$

☐A. 61   ☐B. 50.20

☐C. 60   ☐D. 64.14

STOP

This is the End of this Section. You may check your work on this section if you still have time.

Complete TABE Battery Math Practice Test

Part 2

Applied Mathematics

(Calculator)

50 questions

Total time: 55 Minutes

1) $-18 + 6 \times (-5) - [4 + 22 \times (-4)] \div 2 = ?$

   ☐A. -3 ☐B. 3

   ☐C. -6 ☐D. 6

2) Find the average of the following numbers: $18, 14, 8, 22, 23$

   ☐ A. 17.5   ☐ B. 17

   ☐ C. 16   ☐ D. 10

3) The average of $14, 16, 21$ and x is 20. What is the value of x?

   ☐A. 29   ☐B. 22

   ☐C. 14   ☐D. 4

4) The price of a sofa is decreased by 25% to $471. What was its original price?

   ☐A. $480   ☐B. $520

   ☐C. $560   ☐D. $628

5) If 60% of A is 30% of B, then B is what percent of A?

   ☐A. 2%   ☐B. 20%

   ☐ C. 200%   ☐D. 300%

6) How many possible outfit combinations come from six shirts, two slacks, and five ties?

   ☐A. 60   ☐B. 90

   ☐C. 95   ☐D. 115

7) A writer finishes 160 pages of his manuscript in 20 hours. How many pages is his average?

   ☐ A. 18   ☐ B. 8

   ☐ C. 5   ☐ D. 3

8) The sum of two numbers is M. if one of the numbers is 6, then three times the other number would be what?

   ☐ A. $3M$ ☐ B. $3(M - 6)$

   ☐ C. $3(M + 6)$ ☐ D. $(M - 2)$

9) Which of the following fractions is the largest?

☐ A. $\dfrac{3}{4}$ ☐ B. $\dfrac{2}{5}$

☐ C. $\dfrac{8}{9}$ ☐ D. $\dfrac{2}{3}$

10) If $3x - 6 = 8.5$, What is the value of $5x + 3$?

☐A. 15   ☐B. 15.5

☐C. 20.5   ☐D. 27

11) What is the area of an isosceles right triangle that has one leg that measures $8\ cm$?

☐A. $6\ cm^2$ ☐B. $12\ cm^2$

☐C. $18\ cm^2$ ☐D. $32\ cm^2$

12) A shirt costing \$400 is discounted 15% After a month, the shirt is discounted another 25%. Which of the following expressions can be used to find the selling price of the shirt?

☐A. $(400)(0.60)$ ☐B. $(400) - 400(0.40)$

☐C. $(400)(0.25) - (200)(0.15)$ ☐D. $(400)(0.85)(0.75)$

13) Which of the following points lies on the line with equation $3x + 5y = 11$?

☐A. $(2, 1)$ ☐B. $(-1, 2)$

☐C. $(-2, 2)$ ☐D. $(2, 2)$

14) A taxi driver earns \$8 per 1-hour work. If he works 10 hours a day and in 1 hour he uses 2-liters petrol with price \$1 for 1-liter. How much money does he earn in one day?

☐A. \$90   ☐B. \$88

☐C. \$70   ☐D. \$60

15) When a number is subtracted from 28 and the difference is divided by that number, the result is 3. What is the value of the number?

☐A. 2   ☐B. 4

☐C. 7   ☐D. 12

16) An angle is equal to one fifth of its supplement. What is the measure of that angle?

☐A. 18   ☐B. 24

☐C. 30   ☐D. 45

17) John traveled 150 km in 5 hours and Alice traveled 180 km in 9 hours. What is the ratio of the average speed of John to average speed of Alice?

☐A. 3 : 2   ☐B. 2 : 3

☐C. 5 : 9   ☐D. 9 : 5

18) Right triangle ABC has two legs of lengths 5 cm (AB) and 12 cm (AC). What is the length of the third side (BC)?

☐A. 6 cm   ☐B. 8 cm

☐C. 13 cm   ☐D. 15 cm

19) What is the value of 6^5?

☐A. 7776   ☐B. 2,639

☐C. 855   ☐D. 988

20) 25 is What percent of 50?

☐A. 5%   ☐B. 25%

☐C. 50%   ☐D. 150%

21) The perimeter of the trapezoid below is 54. What is its area?

☐A. 104   ☐B. 120

☐C. 145   ☐D. 150

22) If 45% of a class are girls, and 20% of girls play tennis, what percent of the class play tennis?

☐A. 9%   ☐B. 15%

☐C. 20%   ☐D. 45%

23) The area of a circle is less than 49π. Which of the following can be the circumference of the circle? (Select one or more answer choices)

☐A. 12π ☐B. 14π

☐C. 124π ☐D. 32π

24) What is the value of y in the following system of equation?

$$3x - 4y = -10$$
$$-x + 2y = 10$$

☐A. 10 ☐B. 8

☐C. 6 ☐D. 5

25) In the xy-plane, the point $(4,3)$ and $(3,2)$ are on line A. Which of the following points could also be on line A?

☐A. $(-1,3)$ ☐B. $(5,4)$

☐C. $(3,4)$ ☐D. $(-1,-3)$

26) Two third of 15 is equal to $\frac{2}{5}$ of what number?

☐A. 12 ☐B. 25

☐C. 30 ☐D. 65

27) The marked price of a computer is D dollar. Its price decreased by 25% in January and later increased by 10% in February. What is the final price of the computer in D dollar?

☐A. $0.80\ D$ ☐B. $0.82\ D$

☐C. $0.90\ D$ ☐D. $1.20\ D$

28) A $41 shirt now selling for $29 is discounted by what percent?

☐A. 29% ☐B. 30%

☐C. 40% ☐D. 60%

29) Which of the following could be the product of two consecutive prime numbers?

☐A. 2 ☐B. 10

☐C. 14 ☐D. 35

30) The price of a car was $20,000 in 2014, $15,000 in 2015 and $11,200 in 2016. What is the rate of depreciation of the price of car per year?

☐ A.15%   ☐B. 20%

☐ C. 25%   ☐D. 30%

31) The width of a box is one third of its length. The height of the box is half of its width. If the length of the box is 24 cm, what is the volume of the box?

☐A. 81 cm^3 ☐ B. 162 cm^3

☐C. 243 cm^3 ☐ D. 768 cm^3

32) A bank is offering 5.5% simple interest on a savings account. If you deposit $7,000, how much interest will you earn in five years?

☐A. $360   ☐B. $720

☐C. $1925   ☐D. $3600

33) How many tiles of 8 cm^2 is needed to cover a floor of dimension 4 cm by 24 cm?

☐A. 6   ☐B. 12

☐C. 18   ☐D. 24

34) A rope weighs 600 grams per meter of length. What is the weight in kilograms of 14.2 meters of this rope? (1 $kilograms$ = 1000 $grams$)

☐A. 0.0852   ☐B. 0.852

☐C. 8.52   ☐D. 85.20

35) A chemical solution contains 6% alcohol. If there is 24 ml of alcohol, what is the volume of the solution?

☐A. 240 ml ☐B. 400 ml

☐C. 600 ml ☐D. 1200 ml

36) The average weight of 20 girls in a class is 56 kg and the average weight of 35 boys in the same class is 72 kg. What is the average weight of all the 55 students in that class?

☐A. 60   ☐B. 61.28

☐C. 61.68   ☐D. 66.18

37) The price of a laptop is decreased by 20% to $360. What is its original price?

☐A. 320   ☐B. 380

☐C. 400   ☐D. 450

38) In five successive hours, a car travels $40\ km, 45\ km, 50\ km, 35\ km$ and $55\ km$. In the next five hours, it travels with an average speed of $60\ km\ per\ hour$. Find the total distance the car traveled in 10 hours.

☐A. $425\ km$ ☐B. $450\ km$

☐C. $475\ km$ ☐D.$525\ km$

39) How long does a 420−miles trip take moving at 65 miles per hour (mph)?

☐A. $4\ hours$ ☐B. $6\ hours\ and\ 24\ minutes$

☐C. $7\ hours\ and\ 24\ minutes$ ☐D. $8\ hours\ and\ 30\ minutes$

40) The ratio of boys to girls in a school is $3:2$. If there are 600 students in a school, how many boys are in the school.

☐A. 120   ☐B. 160

☐C. 240   ☐D. 360

41) Sophia purchased a sofa for $530.20. The sofa is regularly priced at $646. What was the percent discount Sophia received on the sofa?

☐A. 12%   ☐B. 18%

☐C. 20%   ☐D. 25%

42) From last year, the price of gasoline has increased from $1.25 per gallon to $1.85 per gallon. The new price is what percent of the original price?

☐A. 72%   ☐B. 120%

☐C. 148%   ☐D. 160%

43) A boat sails 120 miles south and then 50 miles east. How far is the boat from its start point?

☐A. 45 miles   ☐B. 50 miles

☐C. 60 miles   ☐D. 130 miles

44) The score of Emma was half as that of Ava and the score of Mia was twice that of Ava. If the score of Mia was 40 what is the score of Emma?

☐A. 10   ☐B. 15

☐C. 20   ☐D. 40

45) A bag contains 19 balls: three green, five black, eight blue, a brown, a red and one white. If 17 balls are removed from the bag at random, what is the probability that a brown ball has been removed?

☐A. $\frac{1}{19}$ ☐B. $\frac{1}{6}$

☐C. $\frac{16}{17}$ ☐D. $\frac{17}{19}$

46) The average of five consecutive numbers is 48. What is the smallest number?

☐A. 46   ☐B. 36

☐C. 34   ☐D. 12

47) What is the median of these numbers? 5, 10, 14, 9, 16, 19, 6

☐A. 7   ☐B. 10

☐C. 14   ☐D. 16

48) The radius of the following cylinder is 10 inches and its height is 12 inches. What is the surface area of the cylinder in square inches?

☐A. 467.8   ☐B. 342.87

☐C. 104.6   ☐D. 1381.6

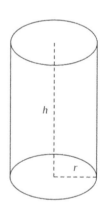

49) In 1989, the average worker's income increased $2,100 per year starting from $25,000 annual salary. Which equation represents income greater than average? (I = income, x = number of years after 1989)

☐A. $I > 2100\,x + 25000$ ☐B. $I > -\,2100\,x + 25000$

☐C. $I < -\,2100\,x + 25000$ ☐D. $I < 2100\,x - 22000$

50) Which graph corresponds to the following inequalities?

$$y \le x + 4$$
$$2x + y \le -4$$

☐A.

☐B.

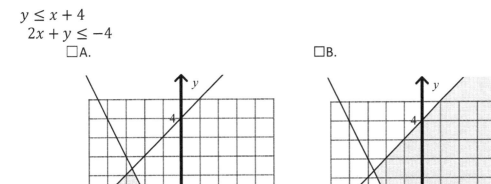

☐C.

☐D.

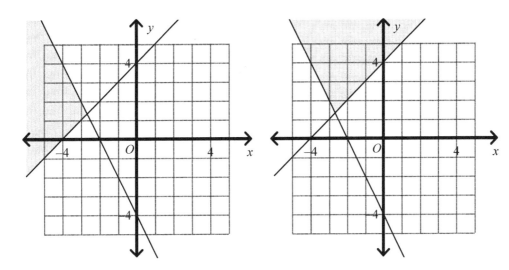

STOP

This is the End of this Section. You may check your work on this section if you still have time.

Complete TABE Battery Math Practice Test Answers and Explanations

❋Now, it's time to review your results to see where you went wrong and what areas you need to improve!

TABE Math Practice Test Answer Key

Parts 1

1-	B	21-	C
2-	D	22-	A
3-	C	23-	D
4-	A	24-	C
5-	C	25-	D
6-	A	26-	A
7-	B	27-	B
8-	D	28-	B
9-	D	29-	A
10-	D	30-	C
11-	D	31-	C
12-	D	32-	C
13-	A	33-	C
14-	C	34-	C
15-	C	35-	C
16-	A	36-	B
17-	D	37-	B
18-	B	38-	A
19-		39-	
20-		40-	

Parts 2

1-	C	21-	A	41-	B
2-	B	22-	A	42-	C
3-	A	23-	A	43-	D
4-	D	24-	A	44-	A
5-	C	25-	B	45-	D
6-	A	26-	B	46-	A
7-	B	27-	A	47-	B
8-	B	28-	D	48-	D
9-	C	29-	C	49-	A
10-	D	30-	D	50-	A
11-	D	31-	C		
12-	D	32-	D		
13-	A	33-	B		
14-	D	34-	C		
15-	C	35-	B		
16-	C	36-	D		
17-	A	37-	D		
18-	C	38-	B		
19-	A	39-	B		
20-	A	40-	D		

Complete TABE Battery Math Practice Test Answers and Explanations

Parts 1: Mathematics Computation

Now, it's time to review your results to see where you went wrong and what areas you need to improve!

1) **Choice B is correct**

   $2,619 - 511 = 2,108$

2) **Choice D is correct**

   $168 + 6,678 = 6,846$

3) **Choice C is correct**

   $760 + 13 = 773$

4) **Choice A is correct**

   $430 - 141 = 289$

5) **Choice C is correct**

   $12 \times 6 = 72$

6) **Choice A is correct**

   $1,383 + 587 = 1,970$

7) **Choice B is correct**

   $8,000 \div 250 = 32$

8) **Choice D is correct**

   $3,521 - 1,563 = 1,958$

9) **Choice D is correct**

   $83.65 + 13.38 = 97.03$

10) **Choice D is correct**

   $5.4 + 4.2 = 9.6$

11) **Choice D is correct**

   $47.12 - 24.34 = 22.78$

12) **Choice D is correct**

$$\begin{array}{r} 6.2 \\ \times\ 3.3 \\ \hline 20.46 \end{array}$$

13) Choice A is correct

$15.6 \div 100 = 0.156$

14) Choice C is correct

$550 \div 5 = 110$

15) Choice C is correct

$\frac{3}{7} + \frac{2}{7} = \frac{5}{7}$

16) Choice A is correct

$12.6 \div 4.6 = 2.7$

17) Choice D is correct

$148 \div 4 = 37$

18) Choice B is correct

$2,768 \div 8 = 346$

19) Choice A is correct

$\frac{4}{3} - \frac{2}{3} = \frac{2}{3}$

20) Choice D is correct

$\frac{4}{5} + \frac{1}{5} = 1$

21) Choice C is correct

$5\frac{3}{2} + 8\frac{1}{3} = 14\frac{5}{6}$

22) Choice A is correct

$6\frac{3}{5} - 2\frac{1}{5} = 6 + \frac{3}{5} - 2 - \frac{1}{5} = 4\frac{2}{5}$

23) Choice D is correct

$5\frac{1}{3} - \frac{3}{4} = 4\frac{7}{12}$

24) Choice C is correct

$\frac{2}{3} \times \frac{5}{7} = \frac{10}{21}$

25) Choice D is correct

$\frac{3}{5} \div \frac{1}{10} = 6$

26) Choice A is correct

$$2\frac{4}{3} \times 2\frac{1}{6} = \frac{10}{3} \times \frac{13}{6} = \frac{130}{18} = 7\frac{2}{9}$$

27) Choice B is correct

$12ab - 7ab = 5ab$

28) Choice B is correct

$4^2 \times 4^5 = 4^{5+2} = 4^7$

29) Choice A is correct

$$4\frac{2}{5} \div 2\frac{6}{10} = \frac{22}{5} \div \frac{26}{10} = \frac{22}{13} = 1\frac{9}{13}$$

30) Choice D is correct

$4\% \text{ of } 20 = 0.04 \times 20 = 0.8$

31) Choice C is correct

$60\% \text{ of } 30 = 0.6 \times 30 = 18$

32) Choice C is correct

$17 - (-14) = 17 + 14 = 31$

33) Choice C is correct

$35\% \text{ of } 40 = 14$

34) Choice C is correct

$8\% \text{ of } \underline{\quad} = 72, \qquad \frac{8}{100} \times x = 72, \qquad \frac{8x}{100} = 72, \qquad x = \frac{7200}{8} = 900$

35) Choice C is correct

$5x + 3x = 8x$

36) Choice B is correct

$10 \times (-3) = -30$

37) Choice B is correct

$8ab - 3ab = 5ab$

38) Choice A is correct

$-3 + 5 + 3 = 5$

39) Choice D is correct

$9^7 \times 9^7 = 9^{14}$

40) Choice D is correct

$160.35 \div 2.50 = 64.14$

Complete TABE Battery Math Practice Test

Answers and Explanations

Parts 2: Applied Mathematics

1) Choice C is correct

Use PEMDAS (order of operation):

$$-18 + 6 \times (-5) - [4 + 22 \times (-4)] \div 2 = -18 - 30 - [4 - 88] \div 2 = -48 - [-84] \div 2$$
$$= -48 + 84 \div 2 = -48 + 42 = -6$$

2) Choice B is correct

$$\frac{18+ 14+8+22+23}{5} = \frac{85}{5} = 17$$

3) Choice A is correct

$$\text{average} = \frac{\text{sum of terms}}{\text{number of terms}} \Rightarrow 20 = \frac{14+16+21+x}{4} \Rightarrow 80 = 51 + x \Rightarrow x = 29$$

4) Choice D is correct

Let x be the original price. If the price of the sofa is decreased by 25% to $471, then:
75 % of $x = 471 \Rightarrow 0.75x = 471 \Rightarrow x = 471 \div 0.75 = 628$

5) Choice C is correct

Write the equation and solve for B: $0.60A = 0.30B$, divide both sides by 0.30, then:

$\frac{0.60}{0.30} A = B$, therefore: $B = 2A$, and B is 2 times of A or it's 200% of A.

6) Choice A is correct

To find the number of possible outfit combinations, multiply number of options for each factor: $6 \times 2 \times 5 = 60$

7) Choice B is correct

$$160 \div 20 = 8$$

8) Choice B is correct

$$x + y = M \rightarrow x = 6 \rightarrow 6 + y = M \rightarrow y = M - 6 \rightarrow 3y = 3(M - 6)$$

9) Choice C is correct

A. $\frac{3}{4} = 0.75$, B. $\frac{2}{5} = 0.4$, C. $\frac{8}{9} = 0.88$, D. $\frac{2}{3} = 0.66$

10) Choice D is correct

$$3x - 6 = 8.5 \rightarrow 3x = 8.5 + 6 = 14.5 \rightarrow x = \frac{14.5}{3} = 4.8$$

Then; $5x + 3 = 5 (4.8) + 3 = 24 + 3 = 27$

11) Choice D is correct

First draw an isosceles triangle. Remember that two sides of the triangle are equal.

Let put a for the legs. Then:

$a = 8 \Rightarrow$ area of the triangle is $= \frac{1}{2} (8 \times 8) = \frac{64}{2} = 32 \ cm^2$

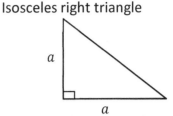
Isosceles right triangle

12) Choice D is correct

To find the discount, multiply the number by $(100\% - rate \ of \ discount)$.

Therefore, for the first discount we get: $(400)(100\% - 15\%) = (400)(0.85)$

For the next 25% discount: $(400)(0.85)(0.75)$

13) Choice A is correct

Plug in each pair of numbers in the equation: $3x + 5y = 11$

A. $(2, 1)$: $3 (2) + 5 (1) = 11$
B. $(-1, 2)$: $3 (-1) + 5 (2) = 7$
C. $(-2, 2)$: $3 (-2) + 5 (2) = 4$
D. $(2, 2)$: $3 (2) + 5 (2) = 16$

Choice A is correct.

14) Choice D is correct

$\$8 \times 10 = \$80 \rightarrow$ Petrol use: $10 \times 2 = 20$ liters $\rightarrow$ Petrol cost: $20 \times \$1 = \$20$

Money earned: $\$80 - \$20 = \$60$

15) Choice C is correct

Let x be the number. Write the equation and solve for x. $(28 - x) \div x = 3$,

Multiply both sides by x.

$(28 - x) = 3x$, then add x both sides. $28 = 4x$, now divide both sides by 4. $x = 7$

16) Choice C is correct

The sum of supplement angles is 180. Let x be that angle. Therefore, $x + 5x = 180$

$6x = 180$, divide both sides by 6: $x = 30$

17) Choice A is correct

The average speed of john is: $150 \div 5 = 30 \ km$

The average speed of Alice is: $180 \div 9 = 20 \ km$

Write the ratio and simplify. $30 : 20 \Rightarrow 3 : 2$

18) Choice C is correct

Use Pythagorean Theorem: $a^2 + b^2 = c^2$

$5^2 + 12^2 = c^2 \Rightarrow 25 + 144 = c^2 \Rightarrow 169 = c^2 \Rightarrow c = 13$

19) Choice A is correct

$6^5 = 6 \times 6 \times 6 \times 6 \times 6 = 7776$

20) Choice A is correct

Use percent formula: $\text{part} = \frac{\text{percent}}{100} \times \text{whole}$

$25 = \frac{\text{percent}}{100} \times 50 \Rightarrow 25 = \frac{\text{percent} \times 50}{100} \Rightarrow 25 = \frac{\text{percent} \times 50}{10}$, multiply both sides by 10.

$250 = \text{percent} \times 50$, divide both sides by 50. $5 = \text{percent}$

21) Choice A is correct

The perimeter of the trapezoid is 54.

Therefore, the missing side (height) is $= 54 - 20 - 12 - 14 = 8$

Area of a trapezoid: $A = \frac{1}{2} h (b_1 + b_2) = \frac{1}{2}(8)(12 + 14) = 104$

22) Choice A is correct

The percent of girls playing tennis is: $45\% \times 20\% = 0.45 \times 0.20 = 0.09 = 9\%$

23) Choices A is correct

Area of the circle is less than 14π. Use the formula of areas of circles.

$Area = \pi r^2 \Rightarrow 49\,\pi > \pi r^2 \Rightarrow 49 > r^2 \Rightarrow r < 7$

Radius of the circle is less than 7. Let's put 7 for the radius. Now, use the circumference formula: $Circumference = 2\pi r = 2\pi\,(7) = 14\,\pi$

Since the radius of the circle is less than 7. Then, the circumference of the circle must be less than 14π. Only choice A is less than 14π.

24) Choice A is correct

Solving Systems of Equations by Elimination

$3x - 4y = -10$
$-x + 2y = 10$ Multiply the second equation by 3, then add it to the first equation.

$\begin{aligned} 3x - 4y &= -10 \\ 3(-x + 2y &= 10) \end{aligned} \Rightarrow \begin{aligned} 3x - 4y &= -10 \\ -3x + 6y &= 30 \end{aligned} \Rightarrow 2y = 20 \Rightarrow y = 10$

25) Choice B is correct

Let x be the number. Write the equation and solve for x.

$\frac{2}{3} \times 15 = \frac{2}{5} \cdot x \Rightarrow \frac{2 \times 15}{3} = \frac{2x}{5}$, use cross multiplication to solve for x.

$5 \times 30 = 2x \times 3 \Rightarrow 150 = 6x \Rightarrow x = 25$

26) Choice B is correct

To find the discount, multiply the number by $(100\% - rate\ of\ discount)$.

Therefore, for the first discount we get: $(D)\ (100\% - 25\%) = (D)\ (0.75) = 0.75\ D$

For increase of 10%: $(0.75\ D)\ (100\% + 10\%) = (0.75\ D)\ (1.10) = 0.82\ D = 82\%\ of\ D$

27) Choice A is correct

Use the formula for Percent of Change: $\dfrac{New\ Value - Old\ Value}{Old\ Value} \times 100\%$

$\dfrac{29-41}{41} \times 100\% = -29\%$ (negative sign here means that the new price is less than old price).

28) Choices D is correct

Some of prime numbers are: $2, 3, 5, 7, 11, 13$

Find the product of two consecutive prime numbers: $2 \times 3 = 6$ (not in the options)

$3 \times 5 = 15$ (not in the options) , $5 \times 7 = 35$ (bingo!) , Choice D is correct.

29) Choice C is correct

Use this formula: Percent of Change: $\dfrac{New\ Value - Old\ Value}{Old\ Value} \times 100\%$

$\dfrac{15000-2000}{20000} \times 100\% = -25\%$ and $\dfrac{11200-15000}{16000} \times 100\% = -25\%$

30) Choice D is correct

If the length of the box is 24, then the width of the box is one third of it, 8, and the height of the box is 4(half of the width). The volume of the box is: $V = lwh = (24)(8)(4) = 768$

31) Choice C is correct

Use simple interest formula: $I = prt$ $(I = interest,\ p = principal,\ r = rate,\ t = time)$

$I = (7,000)(0.055)(5) = 1,925$

32) Choice D is correct

Add the first 5 numbers. $40 + 45 + 50 + 35 + 55 = 225$

To find the distance traveled in the next 5 hours, multiply the average by number of hours.

$Distance = Average \times Rate = 60 \times 5 = 300,$

Add both numbers. $300 + 225 = 525$

33) Choice B is correct

The area of the floor is: $4\ cm \times 24\ cm = 96\ cm^2$

The number of tiles needed $= 96 \div 8 = 12$

34) Choice C is correct

The weight of 14.2 meters of this rope is: $14.2 \times 600\ g = 8520\ g$

$1\ kg = 1,000\ g$, therefore, $8520\ g \div 1000 = 8.52\ kg$

35) Choice B is correct

6% of the volume of the solution is alcohol. Let x be the volume of the solution.

Then: 6% of $x = 24\ ml \Rightarrow 0.06x = 24 \Rightarrow x = 24 \div 0.06 = 400$

36) Choice D is correct

$$\text{average} = \frac{\text{sum of terms}}{\text{number of terms}}$$

The sum of the weight of all girls is: $20 \times 56 = 1120\ kg$

The sum of the weight of all boys is: $35 \times 72 = 2520\ kg$

The sum of the weight of all students is: $1120 + 2520 = 3640\ kg$

$$\text{average} = \frac{3064}{55} = 66.18$$

37) Choice D is correct

Let x be the original price. If the price of a laptop is decreased by 20% to $360, then:

80% of $x = 360 \Rightarrow 0.80x = 360 \Rightarrow x = 360 \div 0.80 = 450$

38) Choice B is correct

Use distance formula: $Distance = Rate \times time \Rightarrow 420 = 65 \times T$, divide both sides by 65. $420 \div 65 = T \Rightarrow T = 6.4\ hours$.

Change hours to minutes for the decimal part. $0.4\ hours = 0.4 \times 60 = 24\ minutes$.

39) Choice B is correct

The equation of a line is in the form of $y = mx + b$, where m is the slope of the line and b is the $y-intercept$ of the line. Two points $(4,3)$ and $(3,2)$ are on line A. Therefore, the slope of the line A is: $slope\ of\ line\ A = \frac{y_2 - y_1}{x_2 - x_1} = \frac{2-3}{3-4} = \frac{-1}{-1} = 1$

The slope of line A is 1. Thus, the formula of the line A is: $y = mx + b = x + b$, choose a point and plug in the values of x and y in the equation to solve for b. Let's choose point $(4, 3)$. Then: $y = x + b \rightarrow 3 = 4 + b \rightarrow b = 3 - 4 = -1$, The equation of line A is: $y = x - 1$

Now, let's review the choices provided:

A. $(-1, 3)$ $y = x - 1 \rightarrow 3 = -1 - 1 = -2$ This is not true.

B. $(5, 4)$ $y = x - 1 \rightarrow 4 = 5 - 1 = 4$ This is true.

C. $(3, 4)$ $y = x - 1 \rightarrow 4 = 3 - 1 = 2$ This is not true.

D. $(-1, -3)$ $y = x - 1 \rightarrow -3 = -1 - 1 = -2$ This is not true!

40) Choice D is correct

Th ratio of boy to girls is $3:2$. Therefore, there are 3 boys out of 5 students. To find the answer, first divide the total number of students by 5, then multiply the result by 3.

$600 \div 5 = 120 \Rightarrow 120 \times 3 = 360$

41) Choice B is correct

The question is this: 530.20 is what percent of 646?

Use percent formula: $part = \frac{percent}{100} \times whole$

$530.20 = \frac{percent}{100} \times 646 \Rightarrow 530.20 = \frac{percent \times 646}{100} \Rightarrow 53020 = percent \times 646 \Rightarrow$

$percent = \frac{53020}{646} = 82.07 \cong 82$

530.20 is 82% of 646. Therefore, the discount is: $100\% - 82\% = 18\%$

42) Choice C is correct

The question is this: 1.85 is what percent of 1.25?

Use percent formula: $part = \frac{percent}{100} \times whole$

$1.85 = \frac{percent}{100} \times 1.25 \Rightarrow 1.85 = \frac{percent \times 1.25}{100} \Rightarrow 185 = percent \times 1.25$

$\Rightarrow percent = \frac{185}{1.25} = 148$

43) Choice D is correct

Use the information provided in the question to draw the shape.

Use Pythagorean Theorem: $a^2 + b^2 = c^2$

$120^2 + 50^2 = c^2 \Rightarrow 14400 + 2500 = c^2 \Rightarrow 16900 = c^2$

$\Rightarrow c = 130$

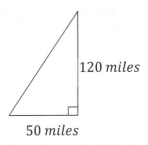

120 miles

50 miles

44) Choice A is correct

If the score of Mia was 40, therefore the score of Ava is 20. Since, the score of Emma was half as that of Ava, therefore, the score of Emma is 10.

45) Choice D is correct

If 17 balls are removed from the bag at random, there will be one ball in the bag.

The probability of choosing a brown ball is 1 out of 19. Therefore, the probability of not choosing a brown ball is 17 out of 19 and the probability of having not a brown ball after removing 17 balls is the same.

46) Choice A is correct

Let x be the smallest number. Then, these are the numbers: $x, x+1, x+2, x+3, x+4$

$$\text{average} = \frac{\text{sum of terms}}{\text{number of terms}} \Rightarrow 48 = \frac{x+(x+1)+(x+2)+(x+3)+(x+4)}{5} \Rightarrow 48 = \frac{5x+10}{5}$$

$$\Rightarrow 240 = 5x + 10 \Rightarrow 230 = 5x \Rightarrow x = 46$$

47) Choice B is correct

Write the numbers in order: $5, 6, 9, 10, 14, 16, 19$

Since we have 7 numbers (7 is odd), then the median is the number in the middle, which is 10.

48) Choice D is correct

Surface Area of a cylinder $= 2\pi r \ (r + h)$,

The radius of the cylinder is 10 inches and its height is 12 inches. π is 3.14. Then:

Surface Area of a cylinder $= 2 \ (3.14) \ (10) \ (10 + 12) \ = 1381.6$

49) Choice A is correct

Let x be the number of years. Therefore, \$2,100 per year equals $2100x$.

starting from \$25,000 annual salary means you should add that amount to $2100x$.

Income more than that is: $I > 2100x + 25000$

50) Choice A is correct

For each option, choose a point in the solution part and check it on both inequalities.
$y \le x + 4$

$2x + y \le -4$

A. Point $(- 4, - 4)$ is in the solution section. Let's check the point in both inequalities.

$- 4 \ \le - 4 + 4$, It works

$2 \ (- 4) + (- 4) \ \le - 4 \Rightarrow - 12 \ \le - 4$, it works (this point works in both)

B. Let's choose this point $(0, 0)$
$0 \ \le 0 + 4$, It works
$2 \ (0) + (0) \ \le - 4$, That's not true!

C. Let's choose this point $(- 5, 0)$
$0 \le - 5 + 4$, That's not true!
D. Let's choose this point $(0, 5)$
$5 \le 0 + 4$, That's not true!

Day 30: A Realistic TABE Math Test

Time to experience a REAL TABE Math Test

Take the following practice TABE Math Test to simulate the test day experience. After you've finished, score your test using the answer key.

Before You Start

- Keep your practice test experience as realistic as possible.

- You'll need a pencil, calculator, and a timer to take the test.

- It's okay to guess. You won't lose any points if you're wrong.

- After you've finished the test, review the answer key to see where you went go.

- **Keep Strict Timing on the Test Section!**

Good Luck!

Mathematics is not only real, but it is the only reality. ~ Martin Gardner

Complete TABE Battery Math

Practice Test

2019

Two Parts

Total number of questions: 90

Part 1 (Non-Calculator) Math Computation: 40 questions

Part 2 (May use Calculator) Applied Math: 50 questions

Total time for two parts: 79 Minutes

Complete TABE Battery Math Practice Test

Part 1

Mathematics Computation

(Non-Calculator)

40 questions

Total time: 24 Minutes

1) $355 + 67 =$

   ☐A. 278   ☐B. 287

   ☐C. 412   ☐D. 422

2)
$$\begin{array}{r} 1{,}215 \\ +\ \ 487 \\ \hline \end{array}$$

   ☐A. 1,623   ☐B. 1,657

   ☐C. 1,690   ☐D. 1,702

3)
$$\begin{array}{r} 2{,}660 \\ -\ \ 623 \\ \hline \end{array}$$

   ☐A. 1,379   ☐B. 1,239

   ☐C. 2037   ☐D. 2,937

4) $\$3{,}558 - \$1{,}245 =$

   ☐A. $1,322   ☐B. $3,803

   ☐C. $1,313   ☐D. $2,313

5) $8 \times 7 =$

   ☐A. 56   ☐B. 72

   ☐C. 81   ☐D. 90

6) $1460 \div 20 =$

   ☐A. 25   ☐B. 56

   ☐C. 73   ☐D. 72

7)
$$\begin{array}{r} 895 \\ +\ \ 45 \\ \hline \end{array}$$

   ☐A. 940   ☐B. 765

   ☐C. 478   ☐D.379

8) $46 \times 5 =$

   ☐A. 155   ☐B. 200

   ☐C. 215   ☐D.230

184

9) 43.35
    + 31.11
    ─────

   ☐A. 744.6   ☐B. 32.45

   ☐C. 74.46   ☐D. 324.5

10) $7.8 - 3.6 =$

   ☐A. 12.4   ☐B. 4.2

   ☐C. 42   ☐D. 124

11)   3.4
    × 3.6
    ─────

   ☐A. 88.10   ☐B. 10.8

   ☐C. 1.80   ☐D. 12.24

12) $15.6 \div 1.3 =$

   ☐A. 1.2   ☐B. 1.5

   ☐C. 12   ☐D. 15

13) $850 \div 5 =$

   ☐A. 17.9   ☐B. 170

   ☐C. 19.6   ☐D. 196

14) $15.5 \div 10 =$

   ☐A. 1.55   ☐B. 15.5

   ☐C. 0.155   ☐D. 0.0155

15) $4\overline{)512}$

   ☐A. 28   ☐B. 113

   ☐C. 128   ☐D. 281

16) $4\overline{)3412}$

   ☐A. 538   ☐B. 853

   ☐C. 865   ☐D. 985

17) $\frac{5}{7} - \frac{2}{7} =$

    □A. $\frac{8}{7}$ □B. $\frac{6}{7}$

    □C. $\frac{3}{7}$ □D. $\frac{1}{7}$

18) $\frac{3}{6} + \frac{1}{2} =$

    □A. $\frac{1}{2}$ □B. $\frac{1}{4}$

    □C. $\frac{2}{4}$ □D. 1

19) $3\frac{4}{3} + 5\frac{1}{3} =$

    □A. $9\frac{2}{3}$ □B. $9\frac{5}{3}$

    □C. $2\frac{1}{3}$ □D. $2\frac{2}{3}$

20) $\frac{3}{2} - \frac{1}{6} =$

    □A. $\frac{1}{3}$ □B. $\frac{4}{3}$

    □C. $\frac{2}{18}$ □D. $\frac{1}{2}$

21) $4\frac{3}{5} - 1\frac{1}{10} =$

    □A. $3\frac{3}{10}$ □B. $3\frac{3}{5}$

    □C. $3\frac{1}{10}$ □D. $3\frac{1}{2}$

22) $\frac{1}{6} \times \frac{5}{12} =$

    □A. $\frac{5}{12}$ □B. $\frac{5}{6}$

    □C. $\frac{3}{5}$ □D. $\frac{5}{72}$

23) $\frac{1}{3} \div \frac{1}{12} =$

☐A. $\frac{3}{4}$ ☐B. $\frac{4}{3}$

☐C. 1   ☐D. 4

24) $1\frac{2}{4} \times 4\frac{1}{8} =$

☐A. $6\frac{3}{16}$ ☐B. $3\frac{5}{8}$

☐C. $3\frac{7}{8}$ ☐D. $5\frac{7}{8}$

25) $7\frac{5}{7} - \frac{1}{2} =$

☐A. $6\frac{4}{7}$ ☐B. $6\frac{2}{7}$

☐C. $7\frac{1}{14}$ ☐D. $7\frac{13}{14}$

26) $17x + 7x =$

☐A. $24x$ ☐B. $9x$

☐C. $3x$ ☐D. $12x$

27) $6^6 \times 6^6 =$

☐A. 6^{12} ☐B. 6^3

☐C. 6^9 ☐D. 6^2

28) $6\frac{2}{4} \div 3\frac{6}{12} =$

☐A. $1\frac{7}{6}$ ☐B. $2\frac{6}{7}$

☐C. $1\frac{6}{7}$ ☐D. $2\frac{7}{6}$

29) 7% of 40

☐A. 2.8   ☐B. 2655

☐C. 26.6   ☐D. 26

30) $5x + 2x =$

☐A. $5 + xx$ ☐B. $5 + 2x$

☐C. $5x$ ☐D. $7x$

31) 30% of 60

☐A. 20 ☐B. 18

☐C. 12 ☐D. 10

32) $14 - (-4) =$

☐A. 4 ☐B. 10

☐C. 14 ☐D. 19

33) ___% of $20 = 15$

☐A. 20% ☐B. 40%

☐C. 75% ☐D. 80%

34) 25% of ___ $= 50$

☐A. 120 ☐B. 180

☐C. 185 ☐D. 200

35) $14xy + 6xy =$

☐A. $6xy$ ☐B. $14xy$

☐C. $16xy$ ☐D. $20xy$

36) $16 \times (-4) =$

☐A. -80 ☐B. -76

☐C. -65 ☐D. -64

37) $-7 + 4 - 5 =$

☐A. -8 ☐B. 8

☐C. -16 ☐D. 16

38) $\sqrt{64}$

    ☐A. 7   ☐B. 8

    ☐C. 9   ☐D. 10

39) $(2 + 2)^2 \div 4 =$

    ☐A. 2   ☐B. 3

    ☐C. 4   ☐D. 5

40) $8x = 4, x = ?$

    ☐A. 4   ☐B. 2

    ☐C. $\dfrac{1}{2}$ ☐D. $\dfrac{1}{4}$

STOP

This is the End of this Section. You may check your work on this section if you still have time.

Complete TABE Battery Math Practice Test

Part 2

Applied Mathematics

(Calculator)

50 questions

Total time: 55 Minutes

1) What is the area of a square whose diagonal is 6?

   ☐A. 18   ☐B. 32

   ☐C. 36   ☐D. 64

2) Anita's trick–or–treat bag contains 15 pieces of chocolate, 10 suckers, 10 pieces of gum, 25 pieces of licorice. If she randomly pulls a piece of candy from her bag, what is the probability of her pulling out a piece of sucker?

   ☐A. $\frac{1}{3}$ ☐B. $\frac{1}{4}$

   ☐C. $\frac{1}{6}$ ☐D. $\frac{1}{12}$

3) Which of the following points lies on the line $x + 2y = 4$? (Select one or more answer choices)

   ☐A. $(-2, 4)$ ☐B. $(1, 2)$

   ☐C. $(-1, 3)$ ☐D. $(-3, 4)$

4) The sum of 8 numbers is greater than 160 and less than 320. Which of the following could be the average (arithmetic mean) of the numbers?

   ☐ A. 10   ☐ B. 20

   ☐ C. 30   ☐ D. 45

5) A tree 32 feet tall casts a shadow 12 feet long. Jack is 8 feet tall. How long is Jack's shadow?

   ☐A. 2.25 ft ☐B. 3 ft

   ☐C. 3.25 ft ☐D. 8 ft

6) What is the product of all possible values of x in the following equation?

   $$|2x - 6| = 10$$

   ☐A. -16 ☐B. -3

   ☐C. 3   ☐D. 16

7) What is the slope of a line that is perpendicular to the line $3x - y = 6$?

   ☐A. -3 ☐B. $-\frac{1}{3}$

   ☐C. 2   ☐D. 6

8) What is the value of the expression $3(x - 2y) + (2 - x)^2$ when $x = 5$ and $= -3$?

☐A. -22 ☐B. 24

☐C. 42   ☐D. 88

9) What is the value of 3^5 ?

☐A. 243   ☐B. 729

☐C. 859   ☐D. 945

10) Which of the following graphs represents the compound inequality $-2 \leq 2x - 4 < 8$?

☐A.

☐B.

☐C.

☐D.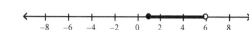

11) What is the volume of a box with the following dimensions?

Hight = 5 cm Width = $6cm$ Length = 7 cm

☐A. 15 cm^3 ☐B. 60 cm^3

☐C. 90 cm^3 ☐D. 210 cm^3

12) Simplify the expression.

$$(7x^3 - 8x^2 + 2x^4) - (4x^2 - 2x^4 + 2x^3)$$

☐A. $4x^4 + 5x^3 - 12x^2$ ☐B. $5x^3 - 12x^2$

☐C. $4x^4 + 5x^3 - 12x^2$ ☐D. $8x^3 - 12x^2$

13) In two successive years, the population of a town is increased by 10% and 20%. What percent of the population is increased after two years?

☐A. 32%   ☐B. 36%

☐C. 38%   ☐D. 58%

14) Last week 25,000 fans attended a football match. This week three times as many bought tickets, but one sixth of them cancelled their tickets. How many are attending this week?

☐A. 48,000   ☐B. 54,500

☐C. 62,500   ☐D. 72,000

15) What is the perimeter of a square in centimeters that has an area of $600.66 \, cm^2$?

☐A. 79.6   ☐B. 98

☐C. 96.7   ☐D. 69.7

16) Which of the following shows the numbers in descending order?

$\frac{2}{3}$, 0.68 , 67% , $\frac{6}{5}$

☐ A. 67%, 0.68, $\frac{2}{3}, \frac{6}{5}$ ☐B. 67%, 0.68, $\frac{6}{5}, \frac{2}{3}$

☐C. 0.68, 67%, $\frac{2}{3}, \frac{6}{5}$ ☐D. $\frac{2}{3}$, 67%, 0.68, $\frac{6}{5}$

17) Which of the following fractions is the largest?

☐ A. $\frac{5}{8}$ ☐ B. $\frac{3}{7}$

☐ C. $\frac{7}{9}$ ☐ D. $\frac{5}{11}$

18) During a fund-raiser, each of the 46 members of a group sold candy bars. If each member sold an average of five candy bars, how many total bars did the group sell?

☐ A. 21   ☐ B. 56

☐ C. 195   ☐ D. 230

19) Which of the following is a multiple of 4?

☐ A. 38   ☐ B. 46

☐ C. 85   ☐ D. 220

20) 55 students took an exam and 22 of them failed. What percent of the students passed the exam?

☐A. 22%   ☐B. 40%

☐C. 60%   ☐D. 80%

21) If 150% of a number is 87, then what is the 90% of that number?

☐A. 45   ☐B. 52.2

☐C. 70.2   ☐D.85

22) What is the slope of the line: $8x - 2y = 6$

☐A. 6   ☐B. 4

☐C. 2   ☐D.1

23) A football team had $25,000 to spend on supplies. The team spent $13,000 on new balls. New sport shoes cost $120 each. Which of the following inequalities represent the number of new shoes the team can purchase.

☐A. $120x + 13,000 \leq 25,000$ ☐B. $120x + 13,000 \geq 25,000$

☐C. $13,000x + 120 \leq 25,000$ ☐D. $13,000x + 12,0 \geq 25,000$

24) $[3 \times (-14) - 48] - (-14) + [3 \times 8] \div 2 = ?$

☐A. 48   ☐B. −48

☐C. 64   ☐D. −64

25) The mean of 50 test scores was calculated as 98. But, it turned out that one of the scores was misread as 94 but it was 69. What is the correct mean of the test scores?

☐A. 85   ☐B.97

☐C. 87.5   ☐D. 97.5

26) Two dice are thrown simultaneously, what is the probability of getting a sum of 6 or 9?

☐A. $\frac{1}{3}$ ☐B. $\frac{1}{4}$

☐C. $\frac{1}{6}$ ☐D. $\frac{1}{12}$

27) The average of five numbers is 25. If a sixth number that is greater than 42 is added, then, which of the following could be the new average?

☐A. 25   ☐B. 26

☐C. 27   ☐D. 28

28) The diagonal of a rectangle is 10 inches long and the height of the rectangle is 6 inches. What is the perimeter of the rectangle in inches?

☐A. 18   ☐B. 28

☐C. 32   ☐D. 35

29) The ratio of boys and girls in a class is $5:6$. If there are 44 students in the class, how many more boys should be enrolled to make the ratio $1:1$?

☐A. 4   ☐B. 10

☐C. 12   ☐D. 14

30) Mr. Jones saves $2,500 out of his monthly family income of $65,000. What fractional part of his income does he save?

☐A. $\frac{1}{26}$ ☐B. $\frac{1}{11}$

☐C. $\frac{3}{26}$ ☐D. $\frac{2}{15}$

31) A swimming pool holds 2,500 cubic feet of water. The swimming pool is 25 feet long and 10 feet wide. How deep is the swimming pool?

☐A. 2   ☐B. 4

☐C. 6   ☐D. 10

32) Mr. Carlos family are choosing a menu for their reception. They have 5 choices of appetizers, 5 choices of entrees, 4 choices of cake. How many different menu combinations are possible for them to choose?

☐A. 20   ☐B. 32

☐C. 60   ☐D. 100

33) In a stadium the ratio of home fans to visiting fans in a crowd is $3:9$. Which of the following could be the total number of fans in the stadium? (Select one or more answer choices)

☐A. 12,336   ☐B. 16,788

☐C. 42,326   ☐D. 44,566

34) The perimeter of a rectangular yard is 72 meters. What is its length if its width is twice its length?

☐A. 12 meters ☐B. 18 meters

☐C. 20 meters ☐D. 24 meters

35) The average of 6 numbers is 14. The average of 4 of those numbers is 10. What is the average of the other two numbers.

☐A. 10 ☐B. 12

☐C. 14 ☐D. 22

36) The perimeter of the trapezoid below is 46 cm. What is its area?

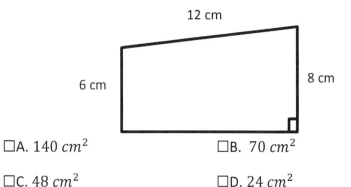

12 cm

6 cm

8 cm

☐A. 140 cm^2 ☐B. 70 cm^2

☐C. 48 cm^2 ☐D. 24 cm^2

37) A card is drawn at random from a standard 78–card deck, what is the probability that the card is of Hearts? (The deck includes 13 of each suit clubs, diamonds, hearts, and spades)

☐A. $\frac{1}{3}$ ☐B. $\frac{1}{4}$

☐C. $\frac{1}{6}$ ☐D. $\frac{1}{78}$

38) Jason needs an 77% average in his writing class to pass. On his first 4 exams, he earned scores of 68%, 72%, 85%, and 90%. What is the minimum score Jason can earn on his fifth and final test to pass?

☐A. 40 ☐B. 60

☐C. 70 ☐D. 75

39) What is the value of x in the following equation?

$$\frac{2}{3}x + \frac{1}{6} = \frac{1}{2}$$

□A. 6　　　　　　　　　　□B. $\frac{1}{2}$

□C. $\frac{1}{3}$　　　　　　　　　□D. $\frac{1}{4}$

40) A bank is offering 3.5% simple interest on a savings account. If you deposit $12,500, how much interest will you earn in two years?

□A. $420　　　　　　　　　□B. $875

□C. $4200　　　　　　　　　□D. $8750

41) Simplify $7x^3y^3(2x^2y)^3 =$

□A. $12x^4y^6$　　　　　　　□B. $12x^8y^6$

□C. $56x^6y^9$　　　　　　　□D. $56x^9y^6$

42) What is the surface area of the cylinder below?

□A. $48\pi\ in^2$　　　　　　　□B. $57\pi\ in^2$

□C. $66\pi\ in^2$　　　　　　　□D. $288\pi\ in^2$

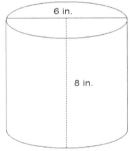

43) The square of a number is $\frac{36}{64}$. What is the cube of that number?

□A. $\frac{6}{8}$　　　　　　　　　□B. $\frac{25}{254}$

□C. $\frac{216}{512}$　　　　　　　　□D. $\frac{125}{64}$

44) What is the median of these numbers? 3,28,29,20,68,45,36

□A. 20　　　　　　　　　　□B. 29

□C. 45　　　　　　　　　　□D. 55

45) A cruise line ship left Port A and traveled 50 miles due west and then 120 miles due north. At this point, what is the shortest distance from the cruise to port A in miles?

☐A. 86   ☐B. 112

☐C. 125   ☐D. 130

46) What is the equivalent temperature of $140°F$ in Celsius?

$$C = \frac{5}{9}(F - 32)$$

☐A. 32   ☐B. 44

☐C. 48   ☐D. 60

47) If 50% of a number is 4, what is the number?

☐A. 4   ☐B. 8

☐C. 10   ☐D. 12

48) The circle graph below shows all Mr. Green's expenses for last month. If he spent $660 on his car, how much did he spend for his rent?

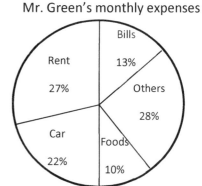

Mr. Green's monthly expenses

☐A. $700   ☐B. $740

☐C. $780   ☐D. $810

49) Jason is 15 miles ahead of Joe running at 5.5 miles per hour and Joe is running at the speed of 7 miles per hour. How long does it take Joe to catch Jason?

☐A. 3 hours   ☐B. 4 hours

☐C. 6 hours   ☐D. 10 hours

50) What is the value of x in the following system of equations?

$$2x + 5y = 17$$
$$4x - 2y = -14$$

☐A. -1 ☐B. 1

☐C. -1.5 ☐D. 1.5

STOP

This is the End of this Section. You may check your work on this section if you still have time.

Complete TABE Battery Math Practice Test Answers and Explanations

✳Now, it's time to review your results to see where you went wrong and what areas you need to improve!

TABE Math Practice Test Answer Key

Parts 1

1- D	21- D		
2- D	22- D		
3- C	23- D		
4- D	24- A		
5- A	25- D		
6- C	26- A		
7- A	27- A		
8- D	28- C		
9- C	29- A		
10- B	30- D		
11- D	31- B		
12- C	32- D		
13- B	33- C		
14- A	34- D		
15- C	35- D		
16- B	36- D		
17- C	37- A		
18- D	38- B		
19- B	39- C		
20- B	40- C		

Parts 2

1- A	21- A	41- D
2- C	22- B	42- C
3- A	23- A	43- C
4- C	24- D	44- B
5- B	25- D	45- D
6- A	26- B	46- D
7- B	27- D	47- B
8- C	28- B	48- D
9- A	29- A	49- D
10- D	30- A	50- C
11- D	31- D	
12- A	32- D	
13- A	33- A	
14- C	34- A	
15- B	35- D	
16- D	36- A	
17- C	37- C	
18- D	38- C	
19- D	39- B	
20- D	40- B	

Complete TABE Battery Math Practice Test Answers and Explanations

Parts 1: Mathematics Computation

1) **Choice D is correct**

   $355 + 67 = 422$

2) **Choice D is correct**

   $$\begin{array}{r} 1{,}215 \\ +\ \ \ 487 \\ \hline 1{,}702 \end{array}$$

3) **Choice C is correct**

   $$\begin{array}{r} 2{,}660 \\ -\ \ \ 623 \\ \hline 2{,}037 \end{array}$$

4) **Choice D is correct**

   $\$3{,}558 - \$1{,}245 = \$2{,}313$

5) **Choice A is correct**

   $8 \times 7 = 56$

6) **Choice C is correct**

   $1460 \div 20 = 73$

7) **Choice A is correct**

   $$\begin{array}{r} 895 \\ +\ \ 45 \\ \hline 940 \end{array}$$

8) **Choice D is correct**

   $46 \times 5 = 230$

9) **Choice C is correct**

   $$\begin{array}{r} 43.35 \\ +\ 31.11 \\ \hline 74.46 \end{array}$$

10) **Choice B is correct**

    $7.8 - 3.6 = 4.2$

11) **Choice D is correct**

$$\begin{array}{r} 3.4 \\ \times\ 3.6 \\ \hline 12.24 \end{array}$$

12) Choice C is correct

$15.6 \div 1.3 = 12$

13) Choice B is correct

$850 \div 5 = 170$

14) Choice A is correct

$15.5 \div 10 = 1.55$

15) Choice C is correct

$512 \div 4 = 128$

16) Choice B is correct

$3,412 \div 4 = 853$

17) Choice C is correct

$\dfrac{5}{7} - \dfrac{2}{7} = \dfrac{3}{7}$

18) Choice D is correct

$\dfrac{3}{6} + \dfrac{1}{2} = 1$

19) Choice B is correct

$3\dfrac{4}{3} + 5\dfrac{1}{3} = 3 + \dfrac{4}{3} + 5 + \dfrac{1}{3} = 9\dfrac{5}{3}$

20) Choice B is correct

$\dfrac{3}{2} - \dfrac{1}{6} = \dfrac{4}{3}$

21) Choice D is correct

$4\dfrac{3}{5} - 1\dfrac{1}{10} = 4 + \dfrac{3}{5} - 1 - \dfrac{1}{10} = 3\dfrac{1}{2}$

22) Choice D is correct

$\dfrac{1}{6} \times \dfrac{5}{12} = \dfrac{5}{72}$

23) Choice D is correct

$\dfrac{1}{3} \div \dfrac{1}{12} = 4$

24) Choice A is correct

$$1\frac{2}{4} \times 4\frac{1}{8} = 1 + \frac{2}{4} + 4 + \frac{1}{8} = 6\frac{3}{16}$$

25) Choice D is correct

$$7\frac{5}{7} - \frac{1}{2} = 7\frac{13}{14}$$

26) Choice A is correct

$$17x + 7x = 24x$$

27) Choice A is correct

$$6^6 \times 6^6 = 6^{12}$$

28) Choice C is correct

$$6\frac{2}{4} \div 3\frac{6}{12} = \frac{13}{2} \div \frac{7}{2} = \frac{26}{14} = 1\frac{6}{7}$$

29) Choice A is correct

7% of 40

$$\frac{7}{100} \times 40 = \frac{280}{100} = 2.8$$

30) Choice D is correct

$$5x + 2x = 7x$$

31) Choice B is correct

$$\frac{30}{100} \times 60 = \frac{1800}{100} = 18$$

32) Choice D is correct

$$14 - (-5) = 19$$

33) Choice C is correct

___% of 20 = 15

$$\frac{x}{100} \times 20 = 15$$

$$x = \frac{1500}{20} = 75\%$$

34) Choice D is correct

25% of ___ = 50

$$\frac{25}{100} \times x = 50$$

$$x = \frac{5000}{25} = 200$$

35) Choice D is correct

$$14xy + 6xy = 20xy$$

36) Choice D is correct

$$16 \times (-4) = -64$$

37) Choice A is correct

$$-7 + 4 - 5 = -8$$

38) Choice B is correct

$$\sqrt{64} = 8$$

39) Choice C is correct

$$(2 + 2)^2 \div 4 = 4$$

40) Choice C is correct

$$8x = 4, x = \frac{1}{2}$$

Complete TABE Battery Math Practice Test

Answers and Explanations

Parts 2: Applied Mathematics

1) Choice A is correct

The diagonal of the square is 6. Let x be the side.

Use Pythagorean Theorem: $a^2 + b^2 = c^2$

$x^2 + x^2 = 6^2 \Rightarrow 2x^2 = 6^2 \Rightarrow 2x^2 = 36 \Rightarrow x^2 = 18 \Rightarrow x = \sqrt{18}$

The area of the square is: $\sqrt{18} \times \sqrt{18} = 18$

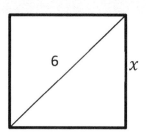

2) Choice C is correct

$$Probability = \frac{number\ of\ desired\ outcomes}{number\ of\ total\ outcomes} = \frac{10}{15+10+10+25} = \frac{10}{60} = \frac{1}{6}$$

3) Choice A is correct

$x + 2y = 6$. Plug in the values of x and y from choices provided. Then:

☐A. $(-2, 4)$ $x + 2y = 4 \rightarrow -2 + 2(4) = 4 \rightarrow -2 + 8 = 6$ This is true!

☐B. $(1, 2)$ $x + 2y = 4 \rightarrow 1 + 2(2) = 4 \rightarrow 1 + 4 = 5$ This is NOT true!

☐C. $(-1, 3)$ $x + 2y = 4 \rightarrow -1 + 2(3) = 4 \rightarrow -1 + 6 = 5$ This is NOT true!

☐D. $(-3, 4)$ $x + 2y = 4 \rightarrow -3 + 2(4) = 4 \rightarrow -3 + 8 = 5$ This is NOT true!

4) Choice C is correct

$\frac{160}{8} < x < \frac{320}{8}$, $20 < x < 40$, From the choices provided, only 30 is correct.

5) Choice B is correct

Write a proportion and solve for the missing number.

$\frac{32}{12} = \frac{8}{x} \rightarrow 32x = 8 \times 12 = 96$, $\quad 32x = 96 \rightarrow x = \frac{96}{32} = 3$

6) Choice A is correct

To solve absolute values equations, write two equations.

$2x - 6$ can equal positive 10, or negative 10. Therefore,

$2x - 6 = 10 \Rightarrow 2x = 16 \Rightarrow x = 8$

$2x - 6 = -10 \Rightarrow 2x = -10 + 6 = -4 \Rightarrow x = -2$

Find the product of solutions: $-2 \times 8 = -16$

7) Choice B is correct

The equation of a line in slope intercept form is: $y = mx + b$

Solve for y. $3x - y = 6 \rightarrow -y = -3x + 6$

Divide both sides by (-1). Then: $-y = -3x + 6 \rightarrow y = 3x - 6$

The slope of this line is 3.

The product of the slopes of two perpendicular lines is -1. Therefore, the slope of a line that is perpendicular to this line is: $m_1 \times m_2 = -1 \Rightarrow 3 \times m_2 = -1 \Rightarrow m_2 = \frac{-1}{3} = -\frac{1}{3}$

8) Choice C is correct

Plug in the value of x and y. $3(x - 2y) + (2 - x)^2$ when $x = 5$ and $y = -3$

$x = 5$ and $y = -3$

$3(x - 2y) + (2 - x)^2 = 3(5 - 2(-3)) + (2 - 5)^2 = 3(5 + 6) + (-3)^2 = 33 + 9 = 42$

9) Choice A is correct

$3^5 = 3 \times 3 \times 3 \times 3 \times 3 = 243$

10) Choice D is correct

Solve for x. $-2 \le 2x - 4 < 8 \Rightarrow$ (add 4 all sides) $-2 + 4 \le 2x - 4 + 4 < 8 + 4 \Rightarrow$

$2 \le 2x < 12 \Rightarrow$ (divide all sides by 2) $1 \le x < 6$

x is between 1 and 6. Choice D represent this inequality.

11) Choice D is correct

$Volume\ of\ a\ box = length \times width \times height = 5 \times 6 \times 7 = 210$

12) Choice A is correct

Simplify and combine like terms. $(7x^3 - 8x^2 + 2x^4) - (4x^2 - 2x^4 + 2x^3) \Rightarrow$
$(7x^3 - 8x^2 + 2x^4) - 4x^2 + 2x^4 - 2x^3 \Rightarrow 4x^4 + 5x^3 - 12x^2$

13) Choice A is correct

the population is increased by 10% and 20%. 10% increase changes the population to 110% of original population. For the second increase, multiply the result by 120%.

$(1.10) \times (1.20) = 1.32 = 132\%$

32 percent of the population is increased after two years.

14) Choice C is correct

Three times of 25,000 is 75,000. One sixth of them cancelled their tickets.

One sixth of 75,000 equals 12,500 ($\frac{1}{6} \times 75000 = 12500$).

62,500 ($75000 - 12500 = 62500$) fans are attending this week

15) Choice B is correct

The area of the square is 600.66. Therefore, the side of the square is square root of the area. $\sqrt{600.66} = 24.5$

Four times the side of the square is the perimeter: $4 \times 24.5 = 98$

16) Choice D is correct

Change the numbers to decimal and then compare.

$\frac{2}{3} = 0.666\ldots, 0.68, 67\% = 0.67, \frac{6}{5} = 1.2$

Therefore: $\frac{2}{3} < 67\% < 0.68 < \frac{6}{5}$

17) Choice C is correct

A. $\frac{5}{8} = 0.625$, B. $\frac{3}{7} = 0.43$, C. $\frac{7}{9} = 0.77$, D. $\frac{5}{11} = 0.45$

18) Choice D is correct

$46 \times 5 = 230$

19) Choice D is correct

A. $\frac{38}{4} = 9.5$, B. $\frac{46}{4} = 11.5$, C. $\frac{85}{4} = 21.25$, D. $\frac{220}{4} = 55$

20) Choice D is correct

The failing rate is 22 out of $55 = \frac{22}{55}$, Change the fraction to percent: $\frac{22}{55} \times 100\% = 40\%$

40 percent of students failed. Therefore, 60 percent of students passed the exam.

21) Choice A is correct

First, find the number. Let x be the number. Write the equation and solve for x.

150% of a number is 87, then: $1.5 \times x = 87 \Rightarrow x = 87 \div 1.5 = 58$

90% of 58 is: $\qquad$ $0.9 \times 58 = 52.2$

22) Choice B is correct

Solve for y. $8x - 2y = 6 \Rightarrow -2y = 6 - 8x \Rightarrow y = 4x - 3$

The slope of the line is 4.

23) Choice A is correct

Let x be the number of new shoes the team can purchase. Therefore, the team can purchase $120\ x$. The team had $25,000 and spent $13,000. Now the team can spend on new shoes $12,000 at most. Now, write the inequality: $120x + 13,000 \leq 25,000$

24) Choice D is correct

Use PEMDAS (order of operation): $[3 \times (-14) - 48] - (-14) + [3 \times 8] \div 2 =$
$[-42 - 48] + 14 + 24 \div 2 = -90 + 14 + 12 = -64$

25) Choice D is correct

average (mean) $= \frac{\text{sum of terms}}{\text{number of terms}} \Rightarrow 98 = \frac{\text{sum of terms}}{50} \Rightarrow sum = 98 \times 50 = 4900$

The difference of 94 and 69 is 25. Therefore, 25 should be subtracted from the sum.

$4900 - 25 = 4875,$ $\qquad$ mean $= \frac{\text{sum of terms}}{\text{number of terms}} \Rightarrow$ mean $= \frac{4875}{50} = 97.5$

26) Choice B is correct

To get a sum of 6 for two dice, we can get 5 different options:

$(5, 1), (4, 2), (3, 3), (2, 4), (1, 5)$

To get a sum of 9 for two dice, we can get 4 different options: $(6, 3), (5, 4), (4, 5), (3, 6)$

Therefore, there are 9 options to get the sum of 6 or 9. Since, we have $6 \times 6 = 36$ total options, the probability of getting a sum of 6 and 9 is 9 out of 36 or $\frac{1}{4}$.

27) Choice D is correct

First, find the sum of five numbers. average $= \frac{\text{sum of terms}}{\text{number of terms}} \Rightarrow 25 = \frac{\text{sum of 5 numbers}}{5}$
$\Rightarrow$ sum of 5 numbers $= 25 \times 5 = 125$

The sum of 5 numbers is 125. If a sixth number that is greater than 42 is added to these numbers, then the sum of 6 numbers must be greater than 167.

$125 + 42 = 167,$ $\qquad$ If the number was 42, then the average of the numbers is:

$$\text{average} = \frac{\text{sum of terms}}{\text{number of terms}} = \frac{167}{6} = 27.83$$

Since the number is bigger than 42. Then, the average of six numbers must be greater than 27.83 . Choice D is greater than 27.83.

28) Choice B is correct

Let x be the width of the rectangle. Use Pythagorean Theorem:

$$a^2 + b^2 = c^2 \rightarrow x^2 + 6^2 = 10^2 \Rightarrow x^2 + 36 = 100$$

$$\Rightarrow x^2 = 100 - 36 = 64 \Rightarrow x = 8$$

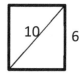

Perimeter of the rectangle = $2\,(length + width) = 2\,(8 + 6) = 2\,(14) = 28$

29) Choice A is correct

Th ratio of boy to girls is $5:6$. Therefore, there are 5 boys out of 11 students. To find the answer, first divide the total number of students by 11, then multiply the result by 5.

$44 \div 11 = 4 \Rightarrow 4 \times 5 = 20$, There are 20 boys and 24 (44 – 20) girls. So, 4 more boys should be enrolled to make the ratio $1:1$

30) Choice A is correct

$2,500$ out of $65,000$ equals to: $\dfrac{2500}{65000} = \dfrac{25}{650} = \dfrac{1}{26}$

31) Choice D is correct

Use formula of rectangle prism volume. $V = (length)(width)(height)$

$$\Rightarrow 2000 = (25)(10)(height) \Rightarrow height = 2500 \div 250 = 10$$

32) Choice D is correct

To find the number of possible outfit combinations, multiply number of options for each factor: $5 \times 5 \times 4 = 100$

33) Choices A is correct

In the stadium the ratio of home fans to visiting fans in a crowd is $3:9$. Therefore, total number of fans must be divisible by $12: 3 + 9 = 12$.

Let's review the choices:

☐A. 12,336: $12,336 \div 12 = 1028$

☐B. 16,789: $16,788 \div 12 = 1,399.88$

☐C. 42,326 $42,326 \div 12 = 3,527.166$

☐D. 44,566 $44,566 \div 12 = 3,713.833$

Only choice A when divided by 12 results a whole number.

34) Choice A is correct

The width of the rectangle is twice its length. Let x be the length. Then, $width = 2x$

Perimeter of the rectangle is $2\,(width + length) = 2(2x + x) = 72 \Rightarrow 6x = 72 \Rightarrow x = 12$

Length of the rectangle is 12 meters.

35) Choice D is correct

average $= \dfrac{\text{sum of terms}}{\text{number of terms}} \Rightarrow$ (average of 6 numbers) $14 = \dfrac{\text{sum of numbers}}{6} \Rightarrow$ sum of 6 numbers is $14 \times 6 = 84$

(average of 4 numbers) $10 = \dfrac{\text{sum of numbers}}{4} \Rightarrow$ sum of 4 numbers is $10 \times 4 = 40$

sum of 6 numbers – sum of 4 numbers = sum of 2 numbers

$84 – 40 = 44$ average of 2 numbers $= \dfrac{44}{2} = 22$

36) Choice A is correct

The perimeter of the trapezoid is $46\ cm$.

Therefore, the missing side (height) is $= 46 – 8 – 12 – 6 = 20$

Area of a trapezoid: $A = \dfrac{1}{2}\,h\,(b_1 + b_2) = \dfrac{1}{2}\,(20)\,(6 + 8) = 140$

37) Choice C is correct

The probability of choosing a Hearts is $\dfrac{13}{78} = \dfrac{1}{6}$

38) Choice C is correct

Jason needs an 77% average to pass for five exams. Therefore, the sum of 5 exams must be at lease $5 \times 77 = 385$

The sum of 4 exams is: $68 + 72 + 85 + 90 = 315$.

The minimum score Jason can earn on his fifth and final test to pass is: $385 – 315 = 70$

39) Choice B is correct

Isolate and solve for x. $\dfrac{2}{3}x + \dfrac{1}{6} = \dfrac{1}{2} \Rightarrow \dfrac{2}{3}x = \dfrac{1}{2} - \dfrac{1}{6} = \dfrac{1}{3} \Rightarrow \dfrac{2}{3}x = \dfrac{1}{3}$

Multiply both sides by the reciprocal of the coefficient of x. $(\dfrac{3}{2})\dfrac{2}{3}x = \dfrac{1}{3}(\dfrac{3}{2}) \Rightarrow x = \dfrac{3}{6} = \dfrac{1}{2}$

40) Choice B is correct

Use simple interest formula: $I = prt$ (I = interest, p = principal, r = rate, t = time)

$I = (12500)(0.035)(2) = 875$

41) Choice D is correct

Simplify. $7x^3y^3(2x^2y)^3 = 7x^3y^3(8x^6y^3) = 56x^9y^6$

42) Choice C is correct

Surface Area of a cylinder = $2\pi r \, (r + h)$,

The radius of the cylinder is 3 ($6 \div 2$) inches and its height is 8 inches. Therefore,

Surface Area of a cylinder = $2\pi \, (3) \, (3 + 8) = 66 \, \pi$

43) Choice C is correct

The square of a number is $\frac{36}{64}$, then the number is the square root of $\frac{36}{64}$, $\sqrt{\frac{36}{64}} = \frac{6}{8}$

The cube of the number is: $(\frac{6}{8})^3 = \frac{216}{512}$

44) Choice B is correct

Write the numbers in order: $3, 20, 28, 29, 36, 45, 68$

Median is the number in the middle. So, the median is 29.

45) Choice D is correct

Use the information provided in the question to draw the shape.

Use Pythagorean Theorem: $a^2 + b^2 = c^2$

$50^2 + 120^2 = c^2 \Rightarrow 2500 + 14400 = c^2 \Rightarrow 16900 = c^2 \Rightarrow c = 130$

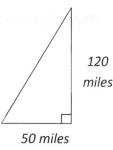

120 miles

Port A

50 miles

46) Choice D is correct

Plug in 140 for F and then solve for C.

$C = \dfrac{5}{9} \, (F - 32) \; \Rightarrow \; C = \dfrac{5}{9} \, (140 - 32) \; \Rightarrow \; C = \dfrac{5}{9} \, (108) = 60$

47) Choice B is correct

Let x be the number. Write the equation and solve for x.

$50\% \ of \ x = 4 \Rightarrow 0.50 \, x = 4 \Rightarrow x = 4 \div 0.50 = 8$

48) Choice D is correct

Let x be all expenses, then $\frac{22}{100}x = \$660 \;\rightarrow\; x = \frac{100 \times \$660}{22} = \$3,000$

He spent for his rent: $\frac{27}{100} \times \$3,000 = \$810$

49) Choice D is correct

The distance between Jason and Joe is 15 miles. Jason running at 5.5 miles per hour and Joe is running at the speed of 7 miles per hour. Therefore, every hour the distance is 1.5 miles less. $15 \div 1.5 = 10$

50) Choice C is correct

Solving Systems of Equations by Elimination

Multiply the first equation by (-2), then add it to the second equation.

$$\begin{array}{l} -2(2x + 5y = 17) \\ \underline{4x - 2y = -14} \end{array} \Rightarrow \begin{array}{l} -4x - 10y = -34 \\ 4x - 2y = -14 \end{array} \Rightarrow -12y = -48 \Rightarrow y = 4$$

Plug in the value of y into one of the equations and solve for x.

$$2x + 5(4) = 17 \Rightarrow 2x + 20 = 17 \Rightarrow 2x = -3 \Rightarrow x = -1.5$$

"Effortless Math Education" Publications

Effortless Math authors' team strives to prepare and publish the best quality TABE Mathematics learning resources to make learning Math easier for all. We hope that our publications help you learn Math in an effective way and prepare for the TABE test.

We all in Effortless Math wish you good luck and successful studies!

Effortless Math Authors

www.EffortlessMath.com

... So Much More Online!

✓ FREE Math lessons

✓ More Math learning books!

✓ Mathematics Worksheets

✓ Online Math Tutors

Need a PDF version of this book?

Visit www.EffortlessMath.com

CPSIA information can be obtained
at www.ICGtesting.com
Printed in the USA
BVHW011923300420
578965BV00011B/263